VISUAL
WORKPLACE
VISUAL THINKING

VISUAL
WORKPLACE
VISUAL THINKING

CREATING ENTERPRISE EXCELLENCE
THROUGH THE TECHNOLOGIES
OF THE VISUAL WORKPLACE

GWENDOLYN D. GALSWORTH

VISUAL-LEAN ENTERPRISE PRESS
PORTLAND, OREGON

Visual-Lean® Enterprise Press

607 NE 32nd Avenue

Portland, Oregon 97232

503-233-1784 (phone)

503-233-3091 (fax)

admin@visualworkplace.com (email)

Galsworth, Gwendolyn D.

ISBN: 1-932516-01-8

Book and Cover Design: William Stanton

Editor: Aurelia Navarro

Printing: PrintSync, Portland, Oregon

Printed in the United States of America

Printing number

9   8   7   6   5   4   3

To the millions of value-add employees who contribute their work lives to companies around the world and who want to do work that makes sense.

AS KINGFISHERS CATCH FIRE

As kingfishers catch fire, dragonflies draw flame;
As tumbled over rim in roundie wells
Stones ring; like each tucked string tells, each hung bell's
Bow swung finds tongue to fling out broad its name.
Each mortal thing does one thing and the same:
Deals out that being indoors each one dwells;
Selves—goes itself; *myself* it speaks and spells,
Crying *What I do is me: for that I came.*

—Gerard Manley Hopkins

CONTENTS

Foreword: Peter Dobbs   xiii

Foreword: Sherrie Ford   xvii

Acknowledgements   xxi

Introduction   1

SECTION ONE   VISUAL BASICS   5

1. **The Visual Workplace and the Excellent Enterprise**   7

   The Solution: Visual Meaning-Visual Performance   10

   Visual Information – Visual Functionality   11

   The Problem: Information Deficits   13

   Information Is Not Performance   16

   Visuality Aligns the Culture   16

   The New Enterprise   20

2. **The Building Blocks of Visual Thinking**   21

   Building Block 1: I-Driven Change   22

   The Two Driving Questions   23

   The Need-to-Know   24

   Workplace Visuality: An I-Driven Approach   27

   The Need-to-Share   29

   Building Block 2: Standards   30

   What Is Supposed to Happen: Standards   30

   Building Block 3: The Six Core Questions   33

   Building Block 4: Information Deficits   36

   Building Block 5: Motion   38

   Motion as the Lever   40

Building Block 6: Work   44

Building Block 7: Value Field   44

Naming the Value Field   45

Building Block 8: Motion Metrics   47

Putting It All Together   48

SECTION TWO   THE CULTURE CONVERSION   53

3. **Leadership and the Power Inversion**   55

The Challenge: Need for a New Paradigm   56

The Big Picture: The Two Pyramids of Power   57

False Decision Point: Which One to Choose?   59

Two Pyramids: Two Functions   59

Pro-Life and Pro-Choice Come to an Agreement   61

The Business Connection   62

Caught in the Middle   63

The How of Empowerment: The Hidden Geometry   64

Liberating the Hidden Pyramid: A Closer Look   65

Participation Myths   66

The Biggest Mistake   70

The Visual Where: Low-Hanging Fruit   71

A Visual Truck Mini-Case Study:

Angie Alvarado: Inverting the Pyramid   73

4. **The I-Driven Culture**   79

Will I Be the Hero of My Own Life?   79

Work Culture: Identity's Mirror   80

The Need to Know: The I-Driven Approach   81

The Phases of the Identity Evolution: From Weak-I to Unified-I   83

Moving Too Quickly to Teams   85

The Visual Remedy: Letting the "I" Drive   87

Rowers, Watchers, Grumblers: Another Perspective on the "I"   93

People are Worth the Pause   95

SECTION THREE   TECHNOLOGIES OF THE VISUAL WORKPLACE   99

5. **Visual Order: Visuality's Foundation**   101

The Goal is Visuality   102

Visual Order (Level 1—Doorway 1)   104

S1: Sort Through/Sort Out   105

S2: Shine The Workplace and Everything in It   107

S3: Secure Safety   110

S4: Select Locations   110

S5: Set Locations   114

The Pattern of Work   115

Customer-Driven Visual Order   122

6. Visual Standards, Displays, and Metrics   129

Visual Standards (Level 2.1—Doorway 2)   131

Visual Displays (Level 2.2—Doorway 3)   133

Visual Metrics and Visual Problem-Solving   140

Visual Metrics (Level 3.1—Doorway 4)   140

Who Owns the Metric?   143

Visual Problem-Solving (Level 3.2—Doorway 4)   146

7. Visual Controls, Guarantees, Machine, Office, & Beyond   151

Visual Controls (Level 4.1—Doorway 5)   152

Strengthening Controls through Design-to-Task   153

Visual Pull Systems (Level 4.2—Doorway 5)   155

Min-Max Levels   155

Kanban/Heijunka   155

Traffic-Light Pull   157

Visual Guarantees (Level 5—Doorway 6)   159

Doorway 6 Owner   163

Doorway 7: The Visual Machine®   165

Doorway 7 Owner   165

Doorway 8: The Visual-Lean® Office   167

A Word about Office Implementations   168

Doorway 9: The Macro-Visual Environment   171

Doorway 10: The Exam-Awards Process   174

SECTION FOUR   VISUAL-LEAN®   179

8. The Visual-Lean Alliance   181

Have You Fully Utilized Visuality?   182

What Lean Contributes   183

What Visual Contributes   184

Critical-Path Visuals vs. Context Visuals   186

Critical-Path Visuals   187

Context Visuals   187

Sustainability   187

The Decision   193

Appendix   197

List of Photos, Photo Albums, Figures & Charts   197

Startup Implementation Template   201

Resources   206

Glossary   219

Index   229

Foreword BY PETER DOBBS

How did you get to work today?

Hundreds of thousands of people travel to work each day, mostly without incident, using a transport system that copes with billons of transactions, supported by little external management. Yet while every single one of us has a unique agenda and set of requirements, as a rule we arrive at our destinations safely and on time, every time, day or night.

All modes of travel face the same challenge with much the same outcome. We find our way around the airport, from departures to passport control, through security and then to the right gate, without asking the way or getting lost. Without speaking a word, we can know, with precision, if our plane is on time, which gate to go to, and when. On the tarmac, planes land and take off in a continuous stream, mostly without incident, despite mind-boggling variables and hair-raising complexity.

The reasons for this are right in front of our eyes—visual information sharing.

Road travel stands witness to the power of visuality as well. Though we may use a map (standard instruction) when we drive, even without one, we receive a vital visual message on average every 3 seconds when travelling at legal speed—and this is excluding the basic white-line road markings. Imagine a road system devoid of all signs, signals, and road markings. Would the billions of transactions each day go as smoothly?

The same is true when we travel by train, bus, underground or any other public transport system. It is the same in the supermarket, gas station, and hospital. Visual devices are everywhere, guiding, informing, instructing, and making us comply. Their value is indisputable and accepted by us all.

Why is it, then, that as soon as we walk through the factory gate or the office door this all goes out the window? The very mechanism that gets us to our destinations, day in and day out, is often ridiculed and treated as "just a few lines on the floor and posters around the shop or office." How many lines and signs got you to where you are today?

I urge every Supervisor, Manager, Director, Vice President, Managing Director, and President to find the time to familiarize themselves with Gwendolyn Galsworth's work and in particular this book, *Visual Workplace–Visual Thinking*. Gwendolyn took me to a new level of "lean thinking" with her unique methodology of not just providing a visual workplace but enabling employees to think differently, to *think visually*.

She gave to the true expert on the shop floor and in the office (the value-add employee) the direct ability to improve his or her own work environment and productivity without the constant support/interference of so-called "lean/process improvement consultants"—outsiders who parachute in, tell those intimately involved in the work how to "do it better", and then disappear, never to be seen again.

This tool of visual thinking clearly belongs with the individual employee, applied by the individual, to the direct benefit of the individual.

I know of no other improvement tool that has this quality or that guarantees such high levels of ownership, self-leadership, and therefore sustainment.

My personal background has had me involved in manufacturing and business process improvement since the early 1970s. I have seen the process grow from Group Technology, Cellular Manufacturing, Systems Engineering, Business Systems Redesign, Lean, and Six Sigma through too many operating systems emulating the acclaimed Toyota Production System. This has been a fabulous journey of learning and application for me that still excites me after 30 years.

I have too many grey hairs and experience to claim that any one of these is better than another. Every improvement strategy is a compilation of tools, and it is the application of these tools at the right time and sequence—aligned with business needs and senior management commitment—that makes a success or failure of any improvement program.

To say, however, that the visual workplace/visual thinking is just another set of tools would be a gross understatement. For me, workplace visuality is not only an extremely powerful tool, it is a compulsory tool, one that must top the list of any business contemplating or going through change.

Why is this? Having taken many companies and factories through the journey to lean, introducing flow, single-point accountability, standardized work, teams, and takt time-based production, visual workplace/visual thinking is the one tool that not only ensures sustainment, it is also a cornerstone of all further improvement opportunities.

Workplace visuality is a powerful tool for enforcing information sharing at the point of use, standardized work, workplace standards, and improved productivity. It also enables employee flexibility, skill-building, and alignment. It drives consistency in operational and financial performance. As Gwendolyn says, "on time, every time, day or night"—using the same methodology that got you where you are sitting today!

Sit back, relax, and start what I believe will be a journey that will take your management abilities and understanding to another level.

Welcome to the Visual Thinking Club!

Peter Dobbs
Vice President Operations, Europe Africa and Middle East
Honeywell Environmental and Combustion Controls

Former Director of Operational Transformation Rolls-Royce plc

Foreword BY SHERRIE FORD

As someone who has worked for two decades in the increasingly distressed trenches called "the shop floor," I can say with confidence that neither training nor improvement strategies rank first in the order of operations for effectively shifting a work culture to meet competitive demand.

My work for decades has involved taking whole work cultures—management, hourly staff, any temps—through an intensive interview process designed to surface what people have lived through as employees, what changes they expect in terms of demand, competition, technology, process, and cost—and finally what changes they would make in the organization in order for it to survive and then excel.

In other words, we ask the organization (and its entire workforce) what is required for effective change to happen there. Every single person in the enterprise is asked to name those top factors (we call them "orders of operations").

In the process of this, we gather hundreds of responses which the employees themselves then analyze, pair, and prioritize through affinity maps and relations diagrams.

We have assisted groups through this process literally hundreds of times in the past 20 years, in every kind of industry and workplace setting. Each and every time we do, the same priorities surface in the top three slots (though terminology and exact order may vary):

- Leadership

- Communication

- Training

Interestingly, all the "usual suspects" for improving performance line up behind them, typically in this order:

- Machine Uptime

- Quality

- More Customers

- Pay and Benefits

The message is clear: What really salvages the enterprise is not what most people start out thinking. The popular improvement tools—six sigma, TPM, concurrent engineering, SPC, the work of Deming, Juran, and Crosby, theory of constraints, gainsharing, customer delight, or takt time, standard work, quick changeover, and other lean tools—all are influenced, driven, governed, strangled, and/or held hostage by leadership, communication, and training.

Note that these top three are culture-making factors, as opposed to throughput considerations. They have the power to salvage an enterprise; they determine whether or not it will respond successfully to the global threats that are closing down companies across the nation. This holds true not just in some industries but in *all* industries.

What does this have to do with *Visual Workplace–Visual Thinking*? I first heard Dr. Galsworth present her concepts at a workshop hosted by Sensormatic in Puerto Rico. As Gwendolyn presented each layer of visual thinking (which must precede visual action), it dawned on me that she has created a methodology that fuses the three culture change drivers—leadership, communication, training—into one.

Beginning with the brilliant concept of creating individual value fields—without which the concept of value streams is less useful—Dr. Galsworth ignites a revolution in the culture mindset. From the individual value field, the culture revolution moves to the team level, the department level, and the enterprise level. Finally, once we have mastered our own visual answers, the revolution moves on to the level of supply chain.

Dr. Galsworth has infused a mastery of the tactics associated with Lean Manufacturing and the Japanese invasion of the 70s–90s with adult learning theory and her own blend of spiritual commentary from a lifetime of studying the meaning of life and the meaning of self. When we divorce operations management from such dimensions, we fail to lead cultures through necessary shifts.

In listening to her ideas, I realized how powerful visual solutions are, particularly the ones that people invent for themselves. I also saw that a device can stand in the place of a supervisor by visually answering questions asked on a day-to-day basis is a far more profound rationale for implementing workplace visuality than "this works for the Japanese; maybe it will work for us." Thanks to the level of visual information they share, these devices can stand in for the team leader, for team members, and even an entire team meeting.

I know because we have begun to undertake this ourselves at Power Partners, a vertically integrated transformer manufacturer. By visually broadcasting streams of information that answer questions on every level, we see that visual information sharing triggers actions systematically around shifts, and eases information deficits that cause performance problems and stresses in the work culture.

If you follow Dr. Galsworth's technologies of the visual workplace, you will automatically achieve improved enterprise performance. The priorities set by the work culture itself, those drawn from the relations diagrams, have proven this.

Here is one of the most compelling paragraphs in the early chapters:

In the pre-visual workplace, everything and everyone is forced to exist within a narrow definition of their capability. The physical work environment is bereft of definition or conveyed context. There is no common purpose. It is devoid of meaning. In their sum, I call these lacks information deficits. Calculating the level of information deficits in your company is the quickest way for you to diagnose the extent to which a visual work environment is both lacking and needed.

And needed—I wish I could convey the experience of watching the input of wave after wave of employees (in mixed sessions, management as well as hourly) that hint at the desperation caused by information deficits. This does not even touch on the enormity of the barriers to trust that these gaps cause—gaps and desperation that the visual workplace is designed to address and correct on the level of each individual.

Workplace visuality starts with *the individual employee*, not with teams, though in time teams evolve and the need for traditional supervisors or foremen dissolves. By starting with the individual employee who masters his or her own value field first, the needed culture sinks deep roots and endures.

In this excellent book, Dr. Galsworth demonstrates how to build a well-informed, well-trained, and spirited work culture where performance results flow naturally. The result will mirror the elusive Toyota culture we strive to copy, a culture born out of an urgency to survive, to experiment, and to capture breakthroughs visually, operator by operator.

There are many beauties to behold in this book: the classification of types of visual devices, the eight building blocks of visual thinking, the ten doorways for creating a visual workplace, and the illustrations (both anecdotal and photographic) of each of these.

The most important lesson I gain from Dr. Galsworth's work, which is captured brilliantly in this book, is that through visual devices of many kinds, we mainline critical information from the production floor or from any place of work, without even knowing we are in dialogue with our space. Floors, walls, machines can be made to lead, tell, train.

In so doing, the number one, two, and three orders of operations for effective culture change are fulfilled. When those are in place, they govern and liberate (not hold hostage) the conditions that make dramatically improved machine uptime, quality, and material flow a reality—along with expanding market share and the promise of long-term employment stability, pay and benefits security, and prosperity for the enterprise and surrounding community.

Sherrie Ford, Ph.D.
Principal
Change Partners

Chairman of the Board and Executive Vice President of Culture
Power Partners, Inc.
Athens, Georgia

Thanks

Acknowledgements

I had tried to write this book for several years but with no success. In the middle of this January, I sat down to try again. It happened, with a press deadline of April 8. For eleven intensive weeks, with one week out for off-site client work, I wrote the book that you are reading now. Needless to say, I did not do it alone.

So many helped. First and foremost are Aurelia Navarro, my editor, Bill Stanton, the book's designer, and Georgia Spence, QMI's new administrative manager (she hadn't been with us more than two weeks before this cyclone hit). These three extraordinarily gifted professionals actually consented to working with me on this absurd schedule—and they did it with remarkable grace and skill.

I will be ever grateful to Bill Stanton for his unfailing aesthetic in the design of the book, brilliantly working out, among many other things, how to present over 200 photographs in a coherent and artful manner—and for the best cover design I could ever ask for. Ever competent and full of good will, Georgia Spence sat in the middle of the cyclone all the time, week in and week out. She did all the initial proofing as well the final preparation of the material before it was sent to Bill; she was a sounding board on nearly every aspect of the book, and somehow kept the office running like a top during it all, even though she was brand new to QMI. I am very lucky.

And Aurelia Navarro, though named as editor, became my teacher from the moment she said yes to the job—at the end of February! Aurelia never wavered in her commitment to keep my voice clear and true, despite some rather eccentric perspectives. She kept me focused and, when the many moments of doubt came—not because of the material but because of the impossible deadline—Aurelia laughed and told me I could do it and it would get done. Every weekend and nearly every night in March was spent at her house, working the chapters, amongst the cats and dog, with her most endearing and adorable Mom, always nearby. Aurelia was a balm on my soul. And I add to these three names Leslie Carver, who joined us after this book was first published and has been extraordinary in her help with the revisions for the second printing.

My admiration and appreciation of these three individuals are without bounds.

I am a very lucky person. I work in a field I love and encounter every day brilliant visual thinkers who share with me (and you) their dazzling inventions. Huge thanks to the many hundreds of individuals who contributed their creativity to this book in the form of their own visual solutions and inventions (some of them used in this book, some in the books to come)—and to the managers, supervisors, and executives who have supported them in this.

Because this book is written for managers, supervisors, and executives, I express a special thanks to you. You are the stewards of the future of your company and the custodians of its current efforts. Your leadership makes a difference every day in the work lives of the people who depend on you—your employees, customers, suppliers, shareholders, and communities.

To those who have allowed us to enter your companies and assist you on the journey to workplace visuality, thank you for your vision, and for your support of excellence before we arrived and after we had completed our work with you.

My thanks, among many many others, to Joseph Linehan, Ken Theiss, Steve Harvey, Paul Baker, Larry Moore, Bill Cornell, Jim Looney, Rick Ell, Dorothy Wall, Sheila Bowersmith, Michael Church, James Justice, Ron and Judy Lake, Dave Dobbins, Gerald Holland, and the entire production team at Parker Denison (formerly Denison Hydraulics); Curt Williams, Matt Furlan, Troy Gerard, and the entire production team at Parker Hannifin; Larry Pike, Mark Swisher, Marty Harnish, Margie Herrara, John Casey, Robert Boykin and the entire production team at Lockheed-Martin; Peter Dobbs of Honeywell; Stephen Pollard, Michael Kern, Robin Tannenburg, and the entire production team at Rolls-Royce; Rick Keller, Donald Van Pelt, Jr., Steve Renforth, and the entire production team at Plymouth Tube; Henk Nooteboom, Marc De Leeuw, Henk Hop, Frank Bogels, Jan Peters, Coby Herman, Max Janssen, Victor Geertruida, and the entire production team at Royal Nooteboom Trailers/Holland; Lars Stenqvist, Henk Heijden, and the entire production team at Scania Trucks/Holland; Tom Wiseman, April Love, and Jason Morin, and the entire production team at Trailmobile/Canada; Beverly Nichols, Rich Mini, John Barrett, Dave Martin, Joyce Clark, and the entire production team at Seton Identification Products; Ronn Page, Carleton Hitchcock, Jonathan Hitchcock, Cindy Krejcha, Mike Suchy, Melanie Haggard, Tim Auelt, Wes Gustafson, Ron Halliday, Adam Koronka, Mike Robbins, Ken Trottier, Troy Zuelzke, and the entire production team at Hitchcock Industries; Dave Reiss, Paul Plant, Bill Antunes, Cindy Barter, Luis Catatao, Bob Comeau, the incomparable John Pacheco, and the entire production team at United Electric Controls; Carol Lepper, Georgia Brown, and Carol Labanco of Midwest Regional Medical Center, Cancer Treatment Centers of America; Armando Botti, Socorro Garza, Mark Brown, and the entire production team at Delphi Deltronicos; Florencia Martinez, and the entire production team at Delphi Rimir; Annie Yu, Kenny Bushmich, George LeVan, Paulette Benedictus, and the entire production team at Skyworks Solutions (formerly Alpha Industries); Angie Alvarado, Frank Lopuzinski, Georgeann Georges, Marv Thaxton, and the entire site and technical team at Sears Parts & Repair Services; Sherrie Ford and Steve Hollis of Power Partners; Wes Eklund, Brett Balkema, and the entire production team at Fleet Engineers; Barry Landon, Mark Metzger, Joseph Wilson, and the entire production team at Schlumberger; John Saathoff, Sue Osier, Janet Jones, Carolyn Rabe, Pat Humke, Larry Penn, Deanna Butler, Beverly Sparks, Buzz Harlan, Melody Sparrow, and the entire production team at Harris Corporation; Jerry Hall, Junior Oliver, Francis Davis, and the entire production team at Delphi Automotive; Jeff Madsen of Wiremold; and Jeff Ellis of Freudenberg-NOK.

For their steadfast support over the years in the tricky business of business, my heartfelt thanks to Dr. Ross Robson and Shaun Barker; Mike Martyn; Dr. Ryuji

Fukuda; Dr. Norman Bodek; Dr. Carol Shaw and Jeanne Steele; Annie Yu; Tom Duffy; Don Guild; Bruce Hamilton; Dr. Robert "Doc" Hall; Dr. Richard Schonberger; Tricia Moody; Joe DeLira; Ron Covington; and Ed Constantine and Lee Alves. And to new business friends who have provided encouragement and insight, Aleta Sherman, Lavon Winkler, Bill West, and Michelle Sobota.

To the QMI Team, in addition to the great Georgia Spence, my sincere appreciation goes to Harald Hope, our webmaster, Jill Pruett, in charge of books, Beth Ann Bennett, our counselor, and Merlin the Cat. And to Mindy Garlington, Angela Willis, and Tina Collins at PrintSync—who always treat us as if we are their only customer.

For the gifts of friendship and care, Kathryn and Andrew Kimball, Diana Brynes, Dawn Bothie, Pamela Thomas, Rania James, Beth Ann Bennett, Jacqueline Miessen, Mataare, Allen Roth, Asarte Reycraft, Annette Mason, Debaura Shantzek, Jan Caviness, Diana Asay, Sara Kane, Anya Nadal, Robert Zubik, Marcy Roban, Sarah Sporn, Elan Clement, Marilynn Considine, Paul Obringer, Barbara Weaver, Clark and Harlean Shea, Rachel Gaffney, Camilla England, Howard Boster, Sharon Ward, and Claude Kennedy. And to my remarkable teacher, Swami Chetanananda.

To my family, for all that you are to me: my brother, Gary Galsworth, my niece, Ondine Galsworth, my nephew, Daniel Spencer Galsworth—and to my parents, Geraldine and Daniel Galsworth, and Mimi Breen who have moved on.

And to Mike Watson, Ron Carbon, and Jessica Wilson—a special thanks and you know why!

And finally my eternal gratitude to Philip Hylos, Samuel Bear, and Anderson Merlin for their wildly creative participation in my life and flawless, unwavering guidance. It is your song I sing.

VISUAL
WORKPLACE
VISUAL THINKING

Introduction

The technologies of the visual workplace represent a comprehensive strategy for installing vital information as close to the point of use as possible. Through this elegant and powerful chain of methods, we eradicate motion—caused by chronic information deficits in the workplace—even as we generate new levels of employee inventiveness and contribution, even as we align the enterprise.

As you will discover by the time you compete this book, workplace visuality creates a set of outcomes that work in parallel with lean outcomes.

Visual builds the details of work into the physical environment and thereby improves adherence, enabling people to work precisely with increasing self-regulation. Lean defines, extends, accelerates, and controls the flow of work that visual spells out, dramatically reducing lead-time and flow distance. Visual imbeds lean gains into the physical workplace and creates self-leadership and alignment on every level of the organization. Visual and lean work hand-in-hand, as do the wings of a bird. Neither is more important; they are of equal importance.

There is understandable confusion on this point because nearly every early training session on lean has a built-in module under the "5S" rubric that teaches the importance of borders and home addresses, two elements of workplace visuality. This leads people to mistakenly assume that the lean approach incorporates visual. It does not.

In fact, as you move through the chapters of this book, you will see that applying 5S solely within the context of lean not only gives implementers a false belief that they are implementing workplace visuality, it also vastly reduces the impact that 5S can contribute to the company's journey to excellence.

In nearly twenty-five years of research and implementation, I have never found an approach more powerful than workplace visuality in liberating, empowering, and aligning the workforce—not just value-add employees but all employees, including managers and executives. And this is only one aspect of its power. From its foundation (5S+1) to visual guarantees (*poka-yoke* systems), the visual workplace is so much more.

Because organizations have an incomplete understanding of the visual approach, they under-implement and therefore under-use the remarkable set of principles, concepts, methods, tools, and practices that constitute the technologies of the visual workplace.

A New Understanding

This book invites you to consider a wholesale upgrade of your vision and understanding of visuality—one that populates the operational landscape with hundreds, even thousands, of visual devices and mini-systems that would redefine entirely, even revolutionize, the way work gets done, waste is reduced, employees are involved, customers are served, and profit is made in your organization.

Imbedded in this invitation is the promise of a new enterprise, one that reaches for and gains excellence as a way of doing business, as part of daily work. That excellence is founded upon the emergence of a new core competency in the corporation, one that I call *visual thinking.*

Visual thinking is the ability of each employee to recognize motion and the information deficits that cause it—and then to eliminate both through solutions that are visual.

Visual thinking, which fits hand-in-glove with lean principles and outcomes, is the doorway to the tomorrow you have been seeking, whatever the industry, whatever the venue.

How to Use this Book

The first in a new series of books on visuality in the workplace, *Visual Workplace –Visual Thinking* focuses on what workplace visuality is, why it is important, and how its fundamental values and premises lead to visual outcomes that are effective, expansive, renewable, and, above all, sustainable.

Ultimately, this is a book about visual thinking and how to create a workforce of visual thinkers. It is written for executives, managers, supervisors, team leaders, and union leadership in its entirety—in short, for anyone and everyone who must work through others to achieve their own objectives.

The second and third books in this new series, *Work That Makes Sense* and *Visuality In Action*, focus on the visual contribution of operators and line employees—the value-add level of the enterprise. Other conceptual and how-to books will follow, addressing such key visual outcomes as visual displays, visual standards, visual metrics and visual problem-solving, visual controls and visual pull systems, and the leadership conversion that the journey to enterprise excellence requires.

My purpose in telling you this is not to take an opportunity to market our other wares but to help you stretch your thinking further about what the visual workplace is and why it is important.

This book is most emphatically *not* an implementation manual, even though it provides many details on the previously misunderstood field of workplace visuality. While it explains what each visual workplace technology is, implementation requires much more detail. What is required is a known sequence of steps that yields early success (the easy part) and ensures long-term sustainability—that elusive holy grail of all improvement activity. The improvement workscape is already littered with too many failed implementations—failed because either the initiative caused more harm than good and/or because improvements did not last.

Primarily, then, this is a book about knowledge, not know-how. It has four sections. Section One focuses on basic concepts and principles, with Chapter 1 discussing enterprise excellence and the pure power of visual information sharing. Chapter 2 presents the eight building blocks of visual thinking and is as close to a methods primer as you will find in this volume.

The second section of the book focuses on the culture of work, beginning with the discussion in Chapter 3 of the role of executives in discovering and developing new facets of leadership—including initiating the empowerment conversion that results in a deeply engaged, spirited, inventive, and aligned workforce. Chapter 4 discusses the evolution of individual employees into visual thinkers, capable of creating a genuinely visual work environment.

The three chapters in the book's third section detail the technologies of the visual workplace, what they are, why they are important, and who takes the lead in implementing them—visual order, visual standards, visual displays, visual metrics, visual problem-solving, visual controls, visual pull systems, and visual guarantees.

The book concludes with a discussion of the visual and lean paradigms, how they support each other, and where the most common mistakes are made in bringing them into alignment—for aligned they must be if excellence in the enterprise is to be achieved and sustained.

Graphics and charts along with over 25 photo albums of actual examples anchor your understanding. Other photographs of visual solutions populate the text. I hope many of these will knock your socks off, much as they knocked off mine when I first saw them.

As you turn the last page, it is my sincere wish that you will have gained a much deeper and more complete understanding of why workplace visuality is crucial to your company's journey to excellence and your own. If all goes well, by book's end, you may also be well on your own way to becoming a visual thinker. I would be so very pleased if you were.

Section | One

VISUAL BASICS

This is a time of great change for all aspects of work, across all industries, on every possible organizational level. The patterns and paradigms of the past no longer serve. Those of the future are not yet in place. We are in a time of transition.

Part of that transition requires a redefinition of what prosperity means and a reformulation of how excellence is achieved in the workplace. A powerful part of that new formula is workplace visuality.

In this section's first chapter, *The Visual Workplace and the Excellent Enterprise*, we will:

- Make broad-stroke distinctions between visual's approach to improvement and that of lean;

- Paint a picture of a fully-functioning visual workplace;

- Name the enemy as *motion* (moving without working) and the *information deficits* that trigger it;

- Describe the remarkable work culture conversion the

visual approach creates, when effectively implemented; and

- Argue in favor of companies launching a visual initiative, even when they have no immediate plans to implement lean.

Chapter 2, *The Building Blocks of Visual Thinking*, focuses entirely on the set of principles and tools fundamental to installing workplace visuality as a new core competency. This set of conceptual elements may appear to be discrete and sequential. It would be more accurate, however, to describe them as a system of elements because of the way they interact and impact each other. In this regard, the eight building blocks represent more of a mindset (a cycle of thinking) than a detailed prescription for improvement action.

We are what we repeatedly do. Excellence,
then, is not an act but a habit.

Aristotle

CHAPTER | **1**

The Visual Workplace and the Excellent Enterprise

The entire world of work—whether factory, hospital, bank, airport, store or government agency—is striving to making work safer, simpler, more logical, more standardized, more fluid, more linked, and less costly. More and more companies are committing to excellence both as the outcome and as the driver of a strategic conversion. This conversion is designed to create prosperity for shareholders, executives, and the workforce itself, as well as for the communities where these organizations are located, and the environment in which they exist.

This is a journey of continuous systematic improvement. Many call this the journey to lean.[1]

The work of the lean journey is to identify and eliminate barriers and constraints in the critical path—the route the material follows as it moves through the company and gains value. The critical path in an organization is comprised of both macro flows of value and hundreds, even thousands, of micro flows. These constitute the value stream.

When a company takes on the work of a lean conversion, it is faced with the need to change or improve or eliminate just about everything under the roof. Achieving lean is a handsome bit of work and the results—the gains—are equally impressive:

- 60%–80% reduction in product flow distance and product time

- 60%–90% reduction in product defects

- Finished goods inventories all but vanish

- WIP levels reduce from days or even weeks to hours

- Productivity levels double, triple, or even quadruple using half the square footage or less

- Batches (and, with them, lead times) slashed to a cycle of one

- And all at a dramatically lower cost and produced in a radically safer environment

Liberated from its former burdens, the company is free to innovate and grow. This is the promise and the actual reality of a lean conversion. What enterprise would not be overjoyed to achieve it?

Yet that self-same enterprise often does not realize—and therefore does not prepare for—the erosion of those gains. Unless specific other steps are systematically undertaken, those hard-won results will deteriorate. It will take a while. Since it took three to five years to convert the production system over to lean, it can take about that long for the gains to evaporate. But it could take less, even as short as a year. Either way, evaporate they will. The heart aches and the pocketbook weeps to see it all go away.

Companies are stunned when this begins to happen. At first, they may attribute the weakening of results to a bad crop of managers or a distraction in the corporate plan. Only after months does the corporation understand that in its rush to lean it neglected one crucial building block of success, the one that would ensure that it lasted: the visual workplace.

The visual workplace is not a brigade of buckets and brooms or posters and signs. It is a compelling operational imperative, central to your war on waste, and crucial to meeting daily performance goals, vastly reduced lead times, dramatically improved quality, and an accelerated sustainable flow—a flow you can control at will.

The visual workplace is the language—the vocabulary—of the lean enterprise made *visual. Workplace visuality*[2] is the sustainment dimension of excellence, the improvement strategy that stabilizes lean gains and keeps them growing.

The same world of work that is rightly enthralled with the promise of lean must now begin to link workplace visuality to that illustrious outcome. Yet most people do not understand the tremendous power of a visual workplace. In not realizing this, they underestimate it, relegating it to the position of an add-on, a mere enhancement or enabler of lean. In this they are mistaken.

The technologies[3] of the visual workplace are, in their sum, a comprehensive methodology for transforming the entire physical workspace and making work safer, simpler, more logical, more standardized, more fluid, more linked, and far less costly—*while ensuring that these outcomes are not just repeatable but sustainable.* As a result, the enterprise becomes increasingly more capable of creating greater and greater prosperity at less cost.

Does this paragraph sound familiar? It should because—except for the italicized phrase in the center—this description of the function of workplace visuality is nearly exactly how, at the start of this chapter, we described the function of lean. Yet visuality is not lean—and lean is not visuality. The two are part of the greater outcome that, for the purposes of this book, I call *The Visual-Lean® Alliance.*

The correct relationship between *visuality* and *lean* is more in keeping with the way wings work on a bird. Both wings are required if the bird is to fly.

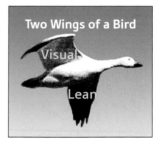

One of the bird's wings represents lean production. The other wing is for workplace visuality. The first wing is about pull, about flow. The second wing is about information, about meaning. Which one is more important? Pull without information? Flow without meaning? Or would you prefer information without pull? A one-winged bird, no matter which wing remains, is no better than a turkey and not nearly as tasty.

FIGURE 1.1:
WINGS OF A BIRD

The enterprise needs them both—pull and information, flow and meaning—if it is to get off the ground and sustain flight. The combined visual-lean outcome is created through the systematic, intentional integration of two closely-allied but importantly distinct sets of concepts, tools, and methods. This is the visual-lean journey.

But we would be mistaken in deciding that visual workplace technologies

> *Management means getting people to do ordinary things extraordinarily well.* —*Ryuii Fukuda*

should be deployed only in companies on the lean journey. We would be incorrect in thinking that only these organizations are ready for or could benefit from a systematic implementation of workplace visuality. In fact, the visual approach to work can be equally, if not more, powerful in a traditional work setting, one that has high-inventory levels, long lead times, quality problems, large batch production, fire-fighting management, and a demoralized workforce.

In fact, workplace visuality can have a major strategic impact in an enterprise that has not yet begun its journey to lean. From many respects, it is most needed there.

What happens when you bring the technologies of the visual workplace powerfully into play in an enterprise that has not yet begun its lean conversion? In 1994, we implemented in just such a facility, a stamping plant in Michigan that had stacks and stacks of inventory when we got there and stacks when we left nearly a year and a half later. Yet during that time, lead time, quality, and on-time delivery had each improved from 15% to 30% throughout the plant and the employee morale—well, let's just say the company finally had one (Photo Album 1).

Should that company have waited until it had implemented lean before pursuing workplace visuality? I don't think so, nor do they nor do you. In many organizations, a strong visual initiative is easier and much more effective to roll out first than lean. Why wait? Start where you are. Start now. Understand where workplace visuality fits in and what it can do for you.

The Solution: Visual Meaning—Visual Performance

What precisely is a visual workplace? Here is the definition we use throughout this book:

> *A visual workplace is a self-ordering, self-explaining, self-regulating, and self-improving work environment—where what is supposed to happen does happen, on time, every time, day or night—because of visual solutions.*

This definition evolved over a decade of implementations and it is worth a close look.

The first half of the definition describes the outcome in terms of functionality:

- The environment will keep itself orderly

- It will explain itself to us

- And, because it can explain itself, it will regulate itself

- Because these are in place, over time, the workplace acquires the ability to correct itself—to become self-improving.

The second half describes a broader outcome: the ability of a visual workplace to reliably and predictably assure the execution of standards—technical and procedural standards—to ensure the means by which the enterprise translates perceived value (what the customer wants) into received value (what the customer buys).

Workplace visuality is a strategy for translating the thousands of informational transactions that transpire every day in the life of the enterprise into visible meaning. This visible meaning doesn't just impact performance; it creates performance.

That's right, the visual workplace is a gigantic adherence mechanism that ensures that what is supposed to happen does happen—on time, every time, day or night—because of visual devices and visual mini-systems.

This must be music to the ears of executives, managers, and supervisors whose primary job it is to help people perform—to help people do what they are supposed to do, time after time after time. That is the central role of the manager. Or, as Dr. Ryuji Fukuda would say: "Management means getting people to do ordinary things extraordinarily well."[4]

Visual Information—Visual Functionality

In a visual workplace, information is converted into simple, universally understood visual devices and installed in the process of work itself, as close to the point of use as possible. The result is the transformation of a formerly mute work environment into one that speaks, eloquently and precisely, about how to use it effectively and efficiently.

What happens when the workplace speaks, when formerly voiceless work stations, equipment, tools, machines, and material can communicate freely with those who use them? What happens when employees can know vital information—the details of work—at-a-glance, without speaking a word, without asking (or answer-

Photo Album 1

The Visual Where at Fleet Engineers

Implementing Workplace Visuality First

Fleet Engineers in Flint, Michigan is a high volume/low mix manufacturer of mud flaps for the trucking industry. Fleet began its journey to excellence by implementing workplace visuality. When the company was ready to tackle the macro flow, the site had a rich application of visuals already in place and a workforce of visual thinkers, poised to take on the challenge.

The Pre-Visual-Lean Workplace ▶

Here is a snapshot of the overall state of the company's macro flow before the launch—piles of WIP and stacks of finished goods inventory.

◀ WIP on Wheels

Fleet's FB-27 Cell was its first visual order showcase. With floor borders in place, the team realized it could put bins of WIP on wheels and do its own material handling—instead of waiting for the single forklift that serviced the entire facility. This small innovation, in the midst of visual, reduced material handling in that cell by 70%.

Double-Function Borders ▶

This double-border function let the FB-27 team tell at-a-glance which product was being worked on—straight on for Product A; slanted for Product B. Such local and particular needs-to-know keep a visual implementation vital and build ever more refined information into the process of work itself.

ing) a single question?

When a work environment becomes a fully-functioning visual workplace, each employee has instant on-demand access to the information needed to do high quality, low cost, timely, and safe work. The workplace is infused with intelligence, visual intelligence that illuminates and drives the corporate intent.

Every section of the floor, every bench, work surface, hand tool, part, machine, rack, cabinet, and bin is equipped to make a contribution to the collective purpose that is beyond its mere existence—because it now can visually communicate vital information to anyone and everyone who needs it, as they need it. There are no exceptions.

In a visual workplace, floors do not exist simply to walk on. Floors are there to help us do our work, repeatedly and with precision. Benches are not merely surfaces on which to place the implements of work. Through *visual order* and the subsequent installation of the *visual where*, floors and benches provide precise visual location information for all the "things" of work.

Through *visual standards* and *visual controls*, tools are not restricted to merely helping us convert material, they also tell us how to use them properly, when they need to be calibrated, and when they are unsafe. They become even more vocal partners in the production process through the technology of *Visual Machine®*— the same visuality that enables equipment to assist in its own quick changeovers. (See *The Four Types/Power Levels of Visual Devices* in Photo Album 2.)

Cells are not merely a collection of functions, things, and people. They are given a voice through *customer-driven visual order*, *visual displays*, and *visual metrics*—and become allies that manage themselves and the enterprise as well.

In a fully-functioning visual workplace, the things of the physical workplace and the workplace itself contribute to the making of profit in ways that go far beyond their mere presence. They become active visual partners in the process of work, in the process of improvement, and in the process of sustaining the gains.

The Problem: Information Deficits

As every company knows, workplace information can change quickly and often— production schedules, customer requirements, engineering specifications, operational methods, tooling and fixtures, material procurement, work-in-process, and the thousand other details on which the daily life of the enterprise depends. In any

Building Adherence through Visuality

Four Power Levels—Types of Visual Devices

A visual device is an apparatus, mechanism, or thing that influences, directs, limits or controls behavior by making information vital to the task at hand available at-a-glance, without speaking a word.

Visual Indicator—No Power ▶

A *Visual Indicator* tells only; it has no power to make us do anything. The 40 mph speed limit sign has no power to make us slow down, any more than these excellent 3-D tabs can make us find the resistors. Both are elective; the choice is ours.

SPEED LIMIT INDICATOR

USEFUL 3-D ADDRESS TABS

Visual Signal—Some Power ▶

A *Visual Signal* first catches our attention, then delivers the message: the simple tactile rumble strip that keeps us from going into the ditch—or set of andon/stacked lights that alerts us to abnormalites.

RUMBLE STRIP

STACKED OR ANDON LIGHTS

Visual Control—Significant Power

A *Visual Control* structures in behavior through size or number. Its power is considerable, as you see in the foam tool delivery system and kanban squares.

SHOP TOOLING

VISUALLY-CONTROLLED TOOL BOXES DESIGNED-TO-TASK

VISUAL PULL SYSTEM KANBAN! ▶

Visual Guarantee—Absolute Power ▶

A *Visual Guarantee* allows the correct response only by embedding exact information into the design of the process itself. These ship stairs require us to start climbing with our right leg (normally the stronger one) and prevents us from skipping steps. A military invention, it ensured that sailors would get topside with all possible speed and safety.

SHIP-SIDE STAIRWAY

single day, literally hundreds of precise data points (information) are required to keep work going. And these data points can and often do change dozens of times every shift. The multiples of these are enormous.

In an information-scarce workplace, people ask lots of questions and lots of the same questions, repeatedly—or they make stuff up. Either way, the company pays in long lead times, late deliveries, poor quality, accidents, low operator and managerial morale, and runaway costs.

Looking across any organization, if workplace visuality is not firmly in place, then these occurrences are not rare. They are chronic and unrelieved. They happen "all the time"—day in/day out, week in/week out, year in/year out. It is a way of life in far too many companies.

In the pre-visual workplace, everything and everyone is forced to exist within a narrow definition of their capability. The physical work environment is bereft of definition or conveyed context. There is no common purpose. It is devoid of meaning. Attempts to improve the process of work invariably fail because even the smallest gains disappear overnight. A pre-visual workplace has no means to sustain them, however hard-won.

This unhappy state of affairs devolves into a single problem: deficits in information. Calculating the level of information deficits in your company (easily described as chronic) is the quickest way for you to diagnose the extent to which a visual work environment is both lacking and needed.

Chronic information deficits—the offices are flooded with them. The production floor is saturated with questions asked and unasked. And sometimes that is even worse. Because when a question exists but never gets asked, people make stuff up. We simply make stuff up. Sometimes that works to the benefit of the company, but all too often it works against it. People make stuff up and accidents happen, material is lost, defects are produced, delivery times are missed, customers flee. Working in an environment without visual information sharing is like trying to reach a destination by driving a hundred miles on a road with no signs, no signals, and no lines down the center of the road. You can probably make it, but you are likely to pay a terrible price.

If yours is already an excellent work environment, you may be tempted to dismiss this scenario as irrelevant to your purposes because environments such as those just described will be out of business soon enough and good riddance.

I am glad your company is doing well. Just be aware that the costs and burdens of those other organizations, suffering in the face of conditions they have yet to address, are your costs as well. These enterprises are your suppliers, your hospital, your Motor Vehicle Department, your trucking company, your schools, and your grocery and department stores. The change must happen with them as well and, until it does, the benefits you reap are limited, at best. We live and work in one world.

Information Is Not Performance

From sales to design, procurement to planning, fabrication to assembly, receiving to pack and ship, and at all points in between, information is the lifeblood of work and all the activities and functions that support work.

In the vast majority of companies, accurate, complete, timely, relevant information is unattainable or simply too hard to come by—and the truth is even harder to locate. That is not to say there aren't plenty of data. Data abound. Data can be found everywhere—in quality reports, SPC graphs, management briefings, in team meetings, and weekly and annual reports. Data flood the workplace.

But compiling data is a fruitless activity if the data are not translated into information and the information is not translated into meaning.

It is meaning that we are after. Without understanding the meaning of the data, we cannot make sound decisions and move the company and the people who work there forward. We cannot *perform*.

The purpose of the visual workplace is to convert data into information, information into visual meaning, and visual meaning into aligned, sustainable performance. If the enterprise is to improve, stabilize, and grow further, this must happen on local and strategic levels.

Visuality Aligns the Culture

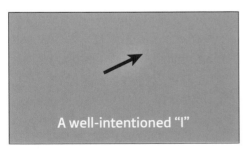

A well-intentioned "I"

FIGURE 1.2: WELL-INTENTIONED "I"

Thinking about company conversions merely in terms of increased production and profits, however, is not just limited; it is useless. Company conversion requires a change that changes everything.

The visual workplace must also be about culture, because when we implement workplace visuality, we liberate information

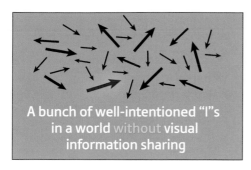

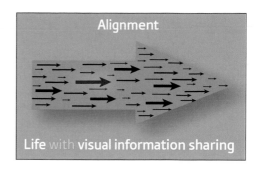

FIGURE 1.3: BUNCH OF "I"s

FIGURE 1.4: ALIGNMENT

in the process. We free vital information that was formerly imprisoned in the binders, reports, books, computer files, and data systems of the company—and in the hearts and minds of that company's information specialists, managers, supervisors, engineers and technicians, and line employees as well. (See Photo Album 3.)

We do this by converting that information into a visible, at-a-glance format for all who need it to access and use. Then—and only then—we can know simply by looking, we can tell merely by looking. And we are free.

Information is power. More than ever before, when we work in a fully-functioning visual workplace, we understand that. Go to work every day in a visual work environment and you cannot help but feel powerful. The information empowers us. We become powerful. When we liberate information, we liberate the human will.

Does this relate to a company's culture? The answer is unequivocally yes. When you have the words information and power in the same sentence, you cannot avoid talking about culture. Culture structures our beliefs and values about two things: power and identity. More specifically, culture reflects how power is used and distributed, and who you think you are and who you think the other person (any other person) is.

In their totality, the technologies of the visual workplace represent over a dozen discrete methods and tools for reducing motion and increasing the visual competency of an organization. Implementing these technologies improves virtually every performance function in the enterprise. Indeed, the continuum of tools contained in these technologies can (and should) be implemented across the company, in all functions, in all departments, in all areas. Once that is firmly in place, move to your sister companies and down your supply chain.

Photo Album 3

Creating a Workforce of Visual Thinkers at RNT

The Visual-Lean® Journey of Royal Nooteboom Trailers

Founded in 1881, Royal Nooteboom Trailers (RNT/Holland) specializes in premium-built specialty trailers, produced by a workforce of over 300 strongly motivated, customer-orientated employees. In 2001, company owner/president Henk Nooteboom launched RNT's journey to excellence with workplace visuality. Eighteen months later, RNT was ready to tackle the challenges of the macro-flow. RNT's visual-lean journey continues to this day.

THE FIRST RNT IMPLEMENTATION GROUP

RNT PRODUCTION FLOOR

THE EURO TRAILER (MULTI-AXLE/LOW LOADER)

DOUBLE-BORDER FUNCTION AT RNT

Rolling Red Tool Box ◣

RNT assembler Berry Voogt raised a simple tool box to a high-level of visuality. He welded it to a pedestal on wheels and put SOPs in a plastic sleeve on the lid—everything he needs handy and at point-of-use.

Victor Invents ◣

With a simple but marvelous inventiveness, Victor Geertruida re-constructed this wrench, making it easier for him to reach tight places. He went on to create many visual solutions.

Kanban Tubes ◣

Max Janssen, assembler and Steering Team member, combined his knowledge of visuality and pull to invent the tube pull location unit above. The green/red markings let him know when more is needed.

The New Enterprise

The new enterprise is an inclusionary entity. It is holistic. As such, it functions on multiple levels, not just meeting the company's daily production goals but also addressing its need for clarity, imagination, community, and alignment. Any effort to make the new enterprise about just one thing, whether production or culture, is a failed concept, unless that concept is unity itself.

The new enterprise, like the human body, must support and express various forms of health—mental, physical, emotional, and, yes, spiritual. It must perform on these multiple levels if it is to remain viable in today's world.

We are on a tremendously accelerated and accelerating journey to a transformation that we can hardly imagine. There is no way to draw the line from where we are now to our future. While there will certainly be familiar signposts, there will also be much that startles and even confounds.

If you haven't noticed it by now, we are in a revolution, not just in manufacturing, not just in offices, not just in hospitals, and not just in the USA. This revolution is taking place in every aspect of lives and livelihood on this planet. It is a revolution of consciousness—and no industry, no country, no company, and no person is exempt.

Chapter 1 Footnotes

1. We will use the term "lean" to refer to the systematic elimination of waste in a company through the application of the principles and tools of the Toyota Production System (TPS), including among others, the quick changeover method (SMED), cellular design, standard work, in-process quality, and takt time.
    These principles apply similarly to outcomes associated with six sigma, ISO, theory of constraints, and other powerful improvement methodologies.
2. My many thanks to Stephen Pollard, good friend and chief business analyst at Rolls-Royce PLC, for coining the term "visuality," and permitting me to adopt it as my own.
3. Chapters 5, 6, and 7 present these technologies in detail, supported by many photographs of actual visual solutions.
4. In no way does this mean that excellent companies prosper only through their capacity to do the same "right thing," repeatedly. On the contrary, forward-moving companies must also find and seize opportunities to do that which has never before been done—to invent, to innovate, to breakthrough. Yet, once an innovation is created, it must be executed, repeatedly and reliably, until it becomes a commonly understood, superbly performed standard. Here workplace visuality functions powerfully.

The worst kind of waste is the waste you don't even see.

Shigeo Shingo

The Building Blocks
of Visual Thinking

A visual workplace is populated by hundreds, even thousands, of visual devices and mini-systems, invented by a workforce that knows how to think visually—a workforce of visual thinkers. What is a *Visual Thinker*?

A visual thinker is a person who recognizes motion and the information deficits that cause it—and knows how to eliminate both through solutions that are visual.

One of the main by-products of effectively implementing the technologies of the visual workplace is the emergence of a new core competency in the enterprise: employees who know how to think visually. Such thinkers see problems in the workplace and solve them from the vantage point of the discrete set of principles called the *Eight Building Blocks of Visual Thinking* (Figure 2.1). This chapter explains each building block and puts it in a strategic context.

Building Block 1: I–Driven Change

There is one simple reason why a visual workplace is needed: People have too many questions. Some of these questions are asked. Most of them remain unasked. When people don't ask the questions, one of two things happens. Either they live without the answers they need and do nothing—or they make stuff up.

Some of what people make up can be useful and does the job. Some of it can be irrelevant or half-wrong, all wrong or, even worse, dangerous. And all that is a problem.

You may wonder why people don't just ask when they don't know. The answer lies in the mysteries of the human heart. Some people don't ask because they don't want to appear uninformed or worse "dumb". Others don't ask because they know that nobody really knows the answer anyway—so why bother. Still others have been lied to (intentionally or otherwise) so often that they don't trust the answers they are given.

Still others refuse to ask because:

a) The question is simple but the answer is unpublished (such as, "What do I do next?")—and that person refuses to ask that level of question over and over again; or

b) The person would have to ask someone half her/his age (or new to the company) who just happens to have the answer. That "someone" is almost always in a position of authority over the person with the question—and the questioner flatly refuses to suffer the indignity of asking a "youngster" or newcomer.

These are not uncommon choices for people to make. Sometimes these two conditions combine so that you are asking the same simple question over and over again of a person half your age. In the face of any of the above, some people will refuse to go after the answers they need and, instead, get angry—or, as mentioned, just make stuff up.

The fact is, many people feel disempowered when asking questions, whereas others feel far too powerful when answering them. One way or the other, asking/answering questions can become a form of power play.

Whatever the motivation or reason, workplace questions that are left unasked and therefore go unanswered can and do cause problems—in safety, quality, cost, on-time delivery, and the great bucket for them all, overall lead time. In a moment,

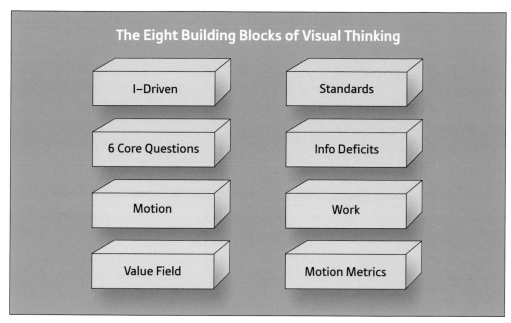

FIGURE 2.1: THE EIGHT BUILDING BLOCKS

we will study some examples.

The Two Driving Questions

*A visual workplace is a self-ordering, self-explaining, self-regulating, and self-improving work environment—where what is **supposed** to happen **does** happen, on time, every time, day or night—**because of visual solutions**.*

The visual workplace is about answering all the questions that anyone has related to work—questions about what is known as well as unknown, questions spoken out loud as well as those on a sub-vocal level, questions that are commonplace as well as those so specialized that others would have never thought, in a million years, to ask such a thing.

To the uninitiated, this sounds a daunting task. To a visual thinker, it is business as usual.

The visual thinker knows that all questions devolve into only two:

Question One: "*What do I need to know?*" What do I need to know that I do not know right now in order to do my work—or do it better? *What do I need to know?*

FIGURE 2.2: THE NEED-TO-KNOW AND NEED-TO-SHARE

Question Two: "*What do I need to share?*" What do I know that others need to know in order for them to do their own work—or do it better? *What do I need to share?*

These two questions drive workplace visuality (Figure 2.2). They make it happen. Once you understand these two questions and get people to apply them, you have practically all the tools you need to achieve a fully-functioning visual workplace that is lastingly sustainable.

The Need-to-Know

The change begins with the need-to-know question: "What do I need to know?" I am always surprised at how plain these "Need-to-Know" questions can be (Inset 2.1). Hank taught me that many years ago. Here's his story.[1]

Hank's Story. Hank worked as an assembler for an electronics manufacturer in the Midwest called, shall we say, Acme Corp. I met Hank along with 35 other operators early in my career at the first Acme training session I conducted for a rollout of workplace visuality there. As usual, early in the session, we discussed the two driving questions; I asked everyone to list out their need-to-know questions. Then I asked for volunteers to share their lists.

Hank, who was sitting in the back of the room, responded first. He didn't bother to raise his hand. He simply started standing up, and as he rose, he repeated the question over and over—"*What do I need to know? What do I need to know?*"—his face getting steadily redder and his voice getting lower and tighter. At full height, Hank leaned

---

INSET 2.1: THE NEED TO KNOW

Here are some need-to-know questions from three organizational levels (across several industries). Notice how plain they are, pointing squarely at the absence of the most fundamental workplace information.

Value-Add Employees

- What am I supposed to run next?
- Where is the fixture for the next changeover?
- When is this claims report due?
- Who runs the session this week?
- How many rooms need to be made up?
- I found the fixture—now how do I do the changeover?

Supervisors/Managers

- Where is the material we've been waiting for?
- When will those sub-assemblies be ready?
- Who's on vacation today?
- How many X-ray plates are left?

These are plain questions that deserve plain and speedy visual answers.

---

forward, rolled his knuckles under, and snarled, "What do I need to know?"

"Yikes! What's going on with this guy," I thought, "Do I have a *crazy* on my hands?" Hank looked as if he would blow at any moment. As the instructor, I ventured forth and drew the fire, "Hey Hank, what do you need to know?" He growled: *"I need to know where my pliers are!"* and brought his hand down on the table hard.

My mouth dropped open; my mind raced: All that upset-ness over a pair of pliers!? I asked for detail. Hank provided it, without missing a beat.

"Listen, I punched in this morning at 6:25 to try to get some stinkin' work done before I had to spend the whole stinkin' morning in this stinkin' class. But I couldn't find my pliers, see! I looked everywhere! *I still don't know where they are!*"

Aaah that explained things! As with the vast majority of a workforce, people come to work *to work*—to make a contribution. That was Hank's intention when he punched in. But to work or even begin to work, Hank needed his pliers. And until he had them in hand, he was stymied.

Hank's work requirement was plain and unadorned. He did not need to know the blueprint to the Death Star or the company's secret acquisition plans. Hank simply wanted to know the location of his pliers so he could get about his work. When I saw Hank's actual list later that morning, the pliers question was the only one on it; his vision stopped there; and he would have no further questions until that one was addressed.

But more happened with Hank that we can learn from. Let me proceed.

As the group and I discussed the need-to-know further, we talked about ways of securing the answers and turning them into visual devices. "In that way," I said, "you never have to ask or answer those particular questions again." Since we were at the very first stage of the journey to visuality, we then talked about *5S+1:Visual Order®*—borders, home addresses, and ID labels—the elements required to attain the *visual where* or, as later explained, *automatic recoil*. The session ended.

A month later I was back on-site at Acme and Hank found me. "Hey, Gwendolyn, guess what happened after you left last time. I tried that border thing you talked about. I decided to put a border on my bench for my pliers (yes, I did eventually find them). And just as I was doing that, Suzie came over. You remember Suzie...."

(Yes, I remembered Suzie: A very pretty woman with a very large mouth. Suzie had a lot of energy that she sometimes used as a weapon to throw a damper on things she didn't like or understand. She was a handful.)

Hank went on. "So Suzie came over and said, 'Hey, what are you doing, Hank?' I told her I was trying out what you talked about in class. And then Suzie just let it rip. 'You have got to be kidding! You are not actually going to try that, are you? Put lines around your pliers? You can't be serious! That'll never help! That's never worked! Anyway, we tried that a few years ago and it didn't work. Don't you remember?'"

"She went on and on, Gwendolyn. She just wouldn't let up."

Hank took a deep breath. "So I took a deep breath and said, 'Suzie, I'm gonna do it anyway! I'm gonna give my pliers a home!' Suzie shot back, 'Well you just go right ahead and do that, Hank. But mark my words: Your pliers will not be there in the morning. Oh I won't touch them! I swear I won't! But they are NOT gonna be there—not in this place! Mark my words!' And she stomped off."

"The next morning, as per usual, I punched at 6:25, went to my bench, and you know what? My pliers weren't there! But guess who was? Yep, Suzie! She was standing there with hands folded across her chest. Before I could say anything, she started in: 'I didn't touch them! I never laid my hands on your pliers! I swear! But I don't see them, do you? I mean I told you they wouldn't be here, right! Right?'"

Hank hung his head in front of me, but his eyes were still sparkling. "Gwendolyn, the pliers were not there. I knew she had me," he said. "Well, I don't know what possessed me to say what I said next, but I said to her, 'Suzie, you are wrong!' That's what I said."

"Suzie blinked at me a couple of times, put her hands on her hips, leaned in real close to my face, and blasted: 'I'm wrong, Hank? How am I wrong, Hank? I mean I don't see your pliers on your bench! Do you? Hank, do you see your pliers? Because I don't! So how am I wrong?'"

Hank continued. "She had me again. And she knew it! But I didn't want to give in. Then BINGO! I got this idea and shot back: 'Suzie, I will tell you why you are wrong. Yesterday it took me 30 minutes to understand that my pliers were gone, really gone. *Today I knew it right away—instantly!*'"

"Suzie's mouth dropped open. 'Huh?' was all that came out of it. Then I got this other thought. 'Suzie,' I said, 'yesterday there was no "there" there! Today there is!'"

"Then the both of us just stood there. I think I was as surprised as she was."

BINGO again! In that short exchange, Hank not only named the true outcome of the process called *5S+1: Visual Order®*[2]—namely installing the *visual where*—he also demonstrated how the question *"What do I need to know?"* drives workplace visuality.

Workplace Visuality: An I-Driven Approach

Note that the question Hank answered reads: "What do *I* need to know?" It does not read: "What do *WE* need to know?"

If it did, Hank would have to meet with the area team (Suzie plus other operators) to discuss the area's need-to-know. Probably the team ("we") would have agreed to make the answers to certain workplace questions visual—but a visual location for Hank's pliers might well have been dismissed as trivial or showing no concrete cost-benefit.

In visual thinking, we deliberately look for ways to make each individual, each person, independent and singular in his or her actions, independent and singular in his or her own improvement ideas. I call this the *I-driven* approach to improvement. To many, this may seem counter-intuitive, the antithesis of creating a unified, team-based work culture. In fact, it is a step in exactly the right direction.

In this first part of the journey to a visual workplace, people are asked to find and follow their own internal improvement goals, their own improvement vision. Although the I-driven approach applies to every employee in the organization, it is most powerfully active with employees on the value-add level (hourly associates,

FIGURE 2.3:
WHAT DO I NEED TO KNOW

The yellow concentric circles here represent the repeat nature of the question/answer process as associates apply and re-apply the need-to-know question to their own individual work. The result is an ever-widening circle of visual devices that captures the answers to work questions, in ever more specific detail, bringing more and more clarity (transparency) and control over their respective corner of the world.

operators, producers or, as Rolls-Royce refers to them, experts) since that is by and large the weakest level in the enterprise for genuine involvement. There, the need for self-referencing is immediate and urgent.

I-driven, this first building block of visual thinking, presses each area associate to take charge of his/her own locus (area) of control and apply the first driving question (need-to-know) as a prod and trigger for populating the work area with visual devices and mini-systems that answer the first question repeatedly—iteratively—question after question after question (Figure 2.3).

There are many impacts that an I-driven approach to change has on enterprise excellence. In our current discussion, I-driven refers to a reliance on and confidence in the individual's need-to-know, on a local level, as the trigger of high-impact/low-cost visual devices and mini-systems.

Among its many other benefits, an I-driven approach to improvement unlinks the need for outside approval or authorization that in the early stages of an initiative can often delay or discourage individual resourcefulness.

Instead of second-guessing outside factors, people are moved by their own inspiration of which visual devices would help them, triggered by their own individual need-to-know.

In the end, every employee has a deep need to be in charge of something. In I-driven visuality, the person declares: "I am in charge of my corner of the world" and behaves accordingly.

There is no way to overemphasize the importance of the I-driven dynamic in creating and sustaining workplace visuality, and ultimately excellence in the enterprise. Indeed, "I-driven" surfaces as a theme again and again in the pages of this book. We have only begun to lay out the reasons why.

INSET 2.2: THE NEED TO SHARE

The need-to-share exists on every organizational level. Used iteratively (repeatedly), its application completes the need for visual answers enterprise-wide.

Value-Add Employees need to share:	**Supervisors/Managers need to share:**
• Where the parts I just ran are now located	• Where I will be this afternoon
• What I am working on now	• What parts get worked on next
• When I will need that report	• When the new parts will arrive
• Who will run this week's session	• What revisions were made
• How many beds are available	
• How many I-Vs were administered this morning	

The Need-to-Share.

When first hearing about the I-driven approach and the first two driving questions, some people worry about anarchy while others comment that this sounds mean-spirited and selfish. Where do other people come in, they wonder. And what about teams? Where do they fit? Where is the "we"?

In creating a visual workplace, other people, teams, and the "we" enter the picture with the second question that drives visuality in the workplace: "What do I need to share?"

That is, *"What do I know that others need to know in order to do their work—or in order to do it better? What information do I need to share?"*

Notice the question is still formed around the "I". It is still I-driven. The focus, however, is now turned outwards to others (Figure 2.4). Reaching out a hand in service, we ask: "How may I help you?" This is a

FIGURE 2.4:
WHAT DO I NEED TO SHARE?

The purple concentric circles here show how the need-to-share reaches beyond local concerns. This ever-widening circle of need-to-share visual devices captures the crucial details that one individual knows and that others need to know in order to perform their work.

deeply team-minded question (Inset 2.2).

Each of us has knowledge and know-how that could be of help to others. When a workforce begins to create visual devices and mini-systems, they start as individuals with an individual need-to-know. This is the foundation of the structure.

After attaining some control over their corner of the world as the result of applying the need-to-know, these same individuals also gain sufficient confidence and command over their local situation to turn to others and begin to share another type of information—the information that they know others need ("What do I need to share?").

In this way, workplace visuality shifts from an individual to a collaborative process, even as the individual continues to retain his/her individuality—the "I."

Building Block 2: Standards

Our definition of a visual workplace states that, in such a work environment, what *is* supposed to happen does happen (Inset 2.3). So we must ask ourselves: what is supposed to happen? What is that thing that *does* happen in a visual workplace?

The answer is: Standards. *A company's standards are supposed to happen, on time, every time, day or night*—and in a visual workplace they do.

What Is Supposed to Happen: Standards

What do we mean by *standards*? When we speak of standards, we are not referring to time or accounting standards used in bids and contracts. We mean the crucial technical and procedural information that defines precisely what value means in the company—and how it is added.

For the purposes of our discussion, there are two categories of standards.

One—Technical Standards: Technical Standards are the dimensions and tolerances of the customer's product and process specifications. These are the values captured in engineering drawings.

Every single object and function in the enterprise is there to meet or support these crucial attributes. Technical standards trigger the full value stream. In fact, they individually and in their aggregate demonstrate what is meant by value in the organization.

INSET 2.3: DEFINITION OF A VISUAL WORKPLACE

A visual workplace is a self-ordering, self-explaining, self-regulating, and self-improving work environment—where what is *supposed* to happen *does* happen, on time, every time, day or night—because of visual solutions.

They are the bedrock, the absolute foundation, of all processes in the corporation—from sales to ordering and procurement; from patient intake to surgery; from incoming deliveries to assembly; from marketing plans to the provision of services. Technical standards (and their execution) form the core of all profit-making in the enterprise (Inset 2.4).

Two—Procedural Standards: Procedural Standards are the pre-determined sequences of steps that ensure that technical specifications are met (as in standard operating procedures or SOPs).

Procedural standards partner with technical standards to create outputs you can sell. Procedural standards refer to exactly how you will achieve your technical standards—those values, dimensions, and specifications (Inset 2.5).

Procedural standards are the step-by-step road map by which you form that 12–inch aluminum ingot into a .50 millimeter thick coil. It is the precise procedure for inserting an I.V. into a patient's arm, and the exact method for programming that CNC machine in the radial department.

INSET 2.4: WHAT IS A TECHNICAL STANDARD?

A *technical standard* refers to the exact tolerance, dimension, specification, or value needed to meet the customer's expectation.

> Examples: *outer diameter (O.D.); inner diameter (I.D.); pressure sensitivity; coil resistance level; cut length; heat-treat temperature; gloss level; torque; required response time on a fire claim; exact degree of radiation for this patient site; dilution level for Taxotere (chemotherapy drug).*

In other words, technical standards describe the precise values of form, fit, and function. They are your product and process specifications.

INSET 2.5: WHAT IS A PROCEDURAL STANDARD?

A *procedural standard* refers to the way in which tasks must be done—methods, standard operating procedures (SOPs). In other words, the sequence of steps we have to follow in order to achieve a specific tolerance, dimension or value (a specific technical standard).

Examples: *How to rivet a bolt; how to achieve a feed rate; how to program the CNC; how to weld; how to tighten a wheel; how to changeover a machine (in less than nine minutes); how to close the monthly books; how to mix and verify a chemotherapy regimen.*

In other words, a Procedural Standard defines *how* to achieve or deliver a specific technical standard. SOPs create outcomes.

The link between technical and procedural standards is as intimate as it is detailed, constituting the precision in what is supposed to happen and how. Your standards are at the heart of operational excellence and reliable, repeatable, cost-effective, high quality work.

Making the details of your standards *visual* is the task of workplace visuality. The visual workplace then becomes a gigantic adherence mechanism that helps us do the right thing, that helps us adhere, and that ensures we execute our standards with exactness.

The absence of clear and complete standards (technical, procedural or both) is a costly deficiency that impacts every single aspect of the organization, in ways that can and cannot be assessed. Any allergy one might have to standards or standardization does not diminish their importance in operational success (Inset 2.6). Yet if an organization lacks precision in this regard, it is not alone. There are many organizations in that same unhappy soup—and in the face of that very deficiency, the technologies of the visual workplace can be of tremendous help to them.

Time and again, companies without documented standards have launched workplace visuality and made vast strides in stabilizing specifications and processes simply through the application of visual principles and tools. One of the beauties of a visual approach is that a company can launch a visual rollout in the absence of known operational standards and, in the process of implementing visuality, put them in place—along with an adherence to them that is both deep-rooted and reliable.

The visual workplace is about information. That is its focus, with visual information sharing the outcome. When we visually share the precise details of what

---

INSET 2.6: ISO AND WORKPLACE VISUALITY—WHEN & WHY

One of the great benefits of committing to ISO certification is the requirement that a company identify and document its technical and procedural standards—every single one of them.

This is an intense task for any company, even those that have stable and consistent standards. For a company that does not have a foundation of standards, the task becomes daunting, often requiring not months but years to complete.

I am often asked if one should initiate ISO first or a visual workplace. Company-by-company differences apply here which may persuade one to begin with ISO, especially if the company is seeking a global market. There is almost no means of delaying that level of mandate.

When given a choice, however, I recommend beginning with an implementation of visual order, the indispensable first step on your journey to a visual workplace.

As you will read in later chapters, there is no shortage of information in a company. The question is: What of it is true—and timely, accurate, complete, and relevant? The question is: Can the workforce access it easily when and as needed?

When you begin your ISO initiative with a rollout of workplace visuality, you can begin to sort out the true from the false and provide a platform for the kind of interpretive research ISO requires. Doing so can reduce the usual time required for ISO certification by 30% to 60%.

Remember: Only the finest manufacturing facilities have completed the groundwork that allows them to know and apply, without hesitation, the details of their technical and procedural standards. All other companies must play catch up.

---

value gets added and how, we are sharing our technical and procedural standards— the *what* in "what is supposed to happen".

Building Block 3: The Six Core Questions

Look closely at technical and procedural standards and notice that they consist of answers to the same set of questions—the same set of six questions. We call these the *Six Core Questions*. They are: Where? What? When? Who? How many? and How?[3]

The answers to these six core questions are the details of the answers to the need-to-know and need-to-share that drive the visual workplace (Figure 2.5).

Yes, that's right: Answer these six questions and you also have the details of your

The Six Core Questions Made Visual

Driving Visuality Through the Six Core Questions

If you knew no other visual concept than the Six Core Questions, you could go far in populating the company with visual answers to them and come very close to achieving a well-functioning visual workplace. They are that powerful.

The Visual Where (floor) ▶
The darkened edges around this floor border & stenciled address reveal a secret: Two coats of sealant can ensure a brightly-defined *visual where* for 18 months or more—even in heavy fork lift traffic. (Fleet Engineers, Flint, MI)

The Visual Where (shelf) ▶

Visual evidence of excellence is every-where at Delphi Deltronicos (Matamoras, Mexico), including inside this HazMat cabinet where the address component of the *visual where* is on a driver-license level—common name, part number, and photo of the thing itself—all the information you need to take value-add action.

◀ The Visual What

This binder of critical assembly operations was compiled by Luis Catatao of United Electric Controls (Watertown, MA) to visually answer exactly "what" the tricky elements were in building switches and controls in his area. While he listed all specs, he only photographed the most critical steps.

◀ The Visual When

Camilla prepared the daily report. Looking for the report each morning, Nate, an engineer, hovered around Camilla making her annoyed. Fine visual thinkers, the two decided to answer the when question (*When will the report be ready?*) with a visual device—the blue bin and red clothespin resulted.

Imagination is Everything

Using the six core questions as drivers does not produce a cookie-cutter result if people are encouraged to use their imaginations. When they do, this process can ignite high levels of diverse and personal inventiveness.

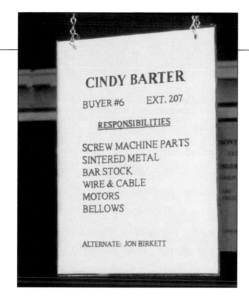

◀ The Visual Who

Cindy Barter at United Electric Controls (Watertown, MA) developed this splendid double-sided airborne address that provides much more than her name in defining the visual who.

The Visual How Many ▶

You can tell at-a-glance that this storage grid at Seton Identification Products (CT) limits the size and height of what fits in each cell as well as the total quantity: 3 deep X 5 long X 1 high. I got it! 15 units!

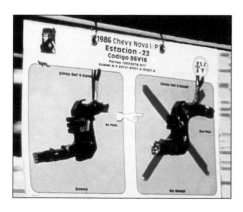

◀ The Visual How

This visual standard (how to tape this harness unit correctly) hung in Rio Bravo IV (Juarez, Mexico) in the mid-1980s when then Packard-Electric (now Delphi Automotive) had just begun its march to excellence. Now, decades later, Delphi is a giant in the industry—and in the field of workplace visuality as well.

The Six Core Questions					
1 Where?	2 What?	3 When?	4 Who?	5 How Many?	6 How?

FIGURE 2.5: THE SIX CORE QUESTIONS

technical and procedural standards. After all, that is all your standards are—over and over again, the answers to the six core questions in precise detail. Answer these questions *visually*—translate them into visual devices—and your standards become built into the process of work and into the environment that supports that process.

The set of six core questions, another visual building block, expresses the synergy between standards, information, and visuality. We focus on making the answers to these six core questions visible—available at-a-glance—and install them as close to the point of use as possible. When we do, the workplace speaks, able at last to tell us where things are, what needs to be done, by when (or for how long), by whom (or by which machine or tool), in what quantity, and precisely how.

See Photo Album 4 for visual answers to the six core questions.

With the six core questions in hand, the task becomes simple: identify the missing answers and install them visually as close to the point of their use as possible. Another term for missing answers is: *Information Deficits*.

Building Block 4: Information Deficits

An information deficit occurs when information vital to the task on hand is missing, wrong, late, unavailable or unknown.

Deficits in information have a vast and disastrous impact on all performance indicators—from quality metrics such as defect and scrap rate, to machine repair and changeover times, to inspection and material handling costs, to accidents and safety-related issues, to cycle time and overall manufacturing lead time. That means that information deficits, by extension, impact the entire business cycle, including sales forecasts and collection activities. Their power is in their absence—the absence of answers.

Information deficits in the workplace trigger costs on every level and, as such, are major profit-eaters. When companies speak of the war on waste, they tend to

---

INSET 2.7: THE FIRST-QUESTION-IS-FREE RULE
Managers Get on Board with Visuality

Questions are one of the most virulent forms of motion, especially on non-value-add levels where managers can sometimes entertain the mistaken notion that their actual job is to answer questions—day in and day out, all the time.

In truth, the need-to-visually-know and -visually-share spans all organizational levels.

I speak to every executive and manager when I say: You can trigger tremendous visual benefit for yourself and the entire enterprise by simply requiring, or even mandating, that your direct reports implement our *First-Question-Is-Free Rule* in their own work and throughout their own value fields. Here's what you tell them:

> *Managers, whenever someone approaches you with a question, answer it politely, truthfully, and as completely as possible.*

> • *For example, Diana may approach in a few moments and ask the question she seems to ask every day at about this time: "Hey, Boss, what am I supposed to do (or make) now?"*

> • *Answer her politely and clearly; and, as she walks away, note inside your head, "That's one."*

> • *Then wait until you are asked that same question again, either by Diana or someone else.*

> • *Again answer the question politely and clearly; and as the person walks away, note inside your head: "That's two!"*

> • *The first question is free; and the second time you hear that same question from the same person or anybody else, it's time for you to create a visual device—so you never ever have to answer that question again and no one has to ask it.*

In requiring this of your direct reports, you will help them undertake what may be their first concrete steps towards becoming leaders of improvement in their area, instead of a manager of fires and other daily calamities.

---

overlook the disastrous impact that missing bits of meaning can produce. Information is the context in which all work happens. If that fabric is full of holes, lots of work, lots of value, escapes.

Most of the time these deficits are so chronic and commonplace, the depth to which they affect organizational performance is nearly impossible to determine. To find them, we must look for their symptom, that which they trigger: motion.

Building Block 5: Motion

The range and extent of information deficits in the workplace are nearly impossible to gauge. We know that they are chronic and widespread, but how do we find them? The answer is to track what they trigger: *Motion.*

In workplace visuality, motion is Corporate Enemy #1. It is defined as: *moving without working.* Motion can take a thousand forms. The easiest way to spot it is to notice when you are wandering about or wondering, searching, asking or answering or any combination of these (Figure 2.6). Doing anything again is another quick way to recognize when you are in motion.

When first learning about motion, people may say, "Yes, but I need to find my pliers to do my work. How can that be motion? How can that be a bad thing? Why is that the enemy?"

Forms of Motion

Searching	Counting
Looking for	Counting again
Wandering	Asking
Wondering	Answering
Guessing	Interrupting
Checking	Waiting
Re-checking	Re-working
Handling	Re-testing
Re-handling	Stopping again & again & again

FIGURE 2.6: FORMS OF MOTION

The answer lies in the fact that when you are looking for your pliers in order to do your work, by definition, you are not working. And that needs to be examined. (See Inset 2.8 for what motion is *not*.)

From that vantage point, you can easily say that motion is anything you *have to do*—anything you are compelled to do—or you *cannot* do your work. Motion is not elective. You do it in order to get back to your work. You have no choice.

- Hank had to find his pliers or he could not assemble the unit.

- Mary was compelled to find the new materials or she could not run the job.

- Victoria, the supervisor, had to re-verify the spec or the job might turn out wrong.

- Ishmael had to count the units again, otherwise he took the chance of shipping the wrong quantity.

- Nurse Betty had to go to the pharmacy to retrieve a pain medication that was late in arriving.

Motion is the plague you don't even see. Tied so intimately and inextricably to

---

INSET 2.8: WHAT MOTION IS NOT

Here is what motion is *not*:

- Taking a break
- Going to lunch
- Calling home
- Going to the restroom
- Chatting with a friend

If you and the workforce do not understand this, people will feel watched and over-regulated; and they will be. One operator said it like this, "I'd feel like a robot, chained to my work bench!"

The activities bulleted above as "not motion" help to create a sense of community, safety, and personal comfort in the workplace, qualifying it as a location for human endeavor.

Dependant on the company, some of the above activities may be regulated, others discretionary. Whatever the case, for the purposes of workplace visuality, none of these are considered forms of motion.

---

unanswered questions (information deficits), motion almost always looks like *business as usual*.

At the outset, only a well-trained pair of improvement eyes can spot the many forms of motion in the workplace. These activities seem so ordinary and so necessary. They are not. Motion eats up the life of the enterprise in the minutia of the micro-transactions we are forced to engage just to get to the starting line of our work—or just to get back to the work itself. It is a numbing experience.

In the chronic absence of fundamental information, employees everywhere—in offices, hospitals, banks, in the field, engineering offices, and on the production floor—become immune to a sense of urgency at work. People become desperate for the simple answers they require to work or continue to work. No one wants to wander around all day, chasing down teeny tiny informational tidbits. It is hard to imagine a more degrading experience or an activity that is more a waste of time. And should these tidbits be held by a select few but withheld from the many, insult gets added to injury. (See Inset 2.9 for more on this, *Information Hoarders*.)

This is not what most people signed up for when they agreed to work for your company. It is not how most people want to earn their daily bread. Simply put, most people want to earn their daily bread in a rightful way. They want to express excellence. In the face of insanity by tidbits, some people go numb; others go ballistic.

The internal dialogue, eyes turned up to Heaven, goes something like this: "Is this what You made me for, dear Lord? This? Chasing down answers to the same old questions, the same ones I asked yesterday, and the day before that, and the day before that? O dear Lord, give me strength!"

For those less religiously-inclined, the inner protest sounds something like: "What the heck is this? Chasing down the same stinkin' answers, day in and day out! I've had it! I'm outta this stinkin' place!"

Neither person may actually quit. Employees on the value-add levels have loved ones to support, mortgages to deal with, bills to pay, and limited alternatives to the job they are doing for you. But make no mistake: They do leave—if only in their minds, if only in their hearts. They make their bodies stay as they consent to a form of modern-day slavery that, to many, is as onerous and soul-bending as the slavery of old.

I see this everywhere when I walk the production floors and offices of the enterprise. People stay. And yet they and we both know that more is possible and wonder why it cannot happen.

That is the destructive power of information deficits (missing information) in the workplace. Motion is merely their symptom.

Motion as the Lever

Every improvement method looks for ways to build a high sense of problem ownership in people. Because information deficits can populate a work environment like grains of sand on a beach, it is easy to make them management's problem on a systems level. When this occurs, however, people quietly disconnect from any responsibility for the problem or for its solution. The problem and the solution are someone else's job. "That's what managers are for," people say.

In a visual workplace, motion is not only corporate enemy #1. It is the main leverage point for making the problem of information deficits detectable and, therefore, for eliminating those deficits and the motion they cause. This is the work of the visual thinker.

The inner discussion goes something like this:

"When I am in motion, it is my own legs that carry me around looking for my pliers; it is my own hands that search through the pile of papers looking for the right work order; it is my own mouth that asks, 'Do you know what I am supposed to do next?' or 'Have you seen my supervisor?'"

Because it is "I" who is doing these things and engaging in these behaviors, I can connect with the fact that there is a problem. I can own the problem as my own. I can identify it and identify with it (here read the word "identify" in two parts, as in I-dentify.)

Understood in this way, motion represents a tremendous advantage if the problem of information deficits is ever to be solved. More than half of the battle in continuous improvement is first getting the workforce to actually own that there is a problem; and then people need to name the problem correctly. Only then can they go after solving it.

In fact, many employees disassociate from problems in the workplace. They either don't see the problem at all, or if they do see it, they expect management to solve it or they blame management for causing it—or both. In paternalistic, traditionally-run companies, most employees do not consider problems as their concern. They

> **INSET 2.9: THE EIGHT DEADLY WASTES VERSUS MOTION**
>
> Here you see the wheel of the seven classic wastes that Toyota has been using for over 30 years—plus one more waste: the opportunities you lose by having to deal with the other seven.
>
> For the reasons explained on this page, we have found it extremely useful to collapse them all into the single waste called motion.
>
>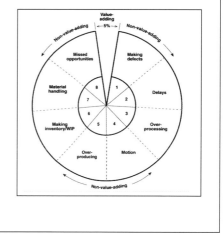

do not own them. Employees in the above scenarios do not see problems as their responsibility, either as something they caused or are able to help solve. This in itself is a huge problem.

Let me say that another way: One of the great challenges in deploying continuous improvement as a strategy in the enterprise is getting people to own workplace problems—and then getting enough people to own them.

When motion (moving without working) is named as the enemy, the company suddenly has a compelling tool for helping people see workplace problems and, once seen, own them. People can I-dentify with motion because they used their own legs, hands, and mouth to search for missing answers. Once I-dentified with motion as the problem, it is so much easier and more natural for people to go down the causal chain and find solutions—visual solutions.

INSET 2.10: INFORMATION HOARDERS—INFORMATION CZARS: A DAMAGING ALTERNATIVE

In far too many companies, information deficits are chronic and widespread. In some, these deficits can become so extreme and persistent that we rightfully ask how the company can stay in business. Part of that answer goes back to the natural resourcefulness of humans and our ability to figure things out and make "stuff" up, however thin the data stream and confusing the circumstances. The other part attests to our willingness to summon up courage and take our best shot. In this, we are both self-serving and heroic.

More times than not, the "stuff" we make up and put in place works, maybe not as well as the actual answer would have, but we get by. And when we do, we add weight to the claim that *people are a company's most important resource.*

In such companies, information deficits can become so habitual that chasing down answers is an expected part of the workday. Some call these *chronic abnormalities.* Perversely, these same workplaces tend to stockpile or even withhold information. This, in turn, can give rise to a new work function—the information hoarders, always a double-edged sword.

Whether formalized into an actual position (e.g., expediter) or simply the informal *go-to person* (the one in the know), information hoarders erode the culture of the enterprise. They represent an unofficial system, put in place to make the official systems work, or work better. In such organizations, no decision is final until informal (and more reliable) sources have validated its wisdom. Information-based fiefdoms emerge that a company can come to depend on as the only reliable source, giving rise to information czars.

Information hoarders represent a damaging alternative when information vital to work and sound decision-making is scarce, wrong, unavailable, irrelevant, incomplete, unreliable, late or just plain unknowable. This is a work environment that tells lies—lies to itself and others. They are the people we go to to learn the truth—what's really happening, what's really going on, what's really required, what's really in the forecast. Being the single trustee of the truth is simply too much power for any to hold; and when this power resides in one special person or one special group, whatever their intentions, the rest of us become disempowered.

Information hoarders in the enterprise are almost always a sign of trouble—but not the trouble itself. The trouble itself is the existence of information deficits. Such an environment (and I find them everywhere) is destructive to a fundamental requirement of the workplace: our need for the truth and our need to trust the information we are given as the truth. The upshot is an incapable, unstable production system that creates value at the highest possible cost.

When the time comes to initiate a change, the task becomes doubly difficult and doubly important if information hoarders are already deeply imbedded in the fabric of the workplace.

You may be wondering why I do not use more common terms for naming the enemy—*muda*, waste, or non-value-adding activity (Inset 2.9). My decision *not* to use these was made many years back. I believe you will understand the reasons.

1. **Muda:** *Muda* is not an English word; it has no meaning except in its translation. When given a choice, I prefer to use an English language equivalent to foreign language terms.

2. **Waste:** The term "waste" is very broad. Although it can be useful for just that reason—to generalize the problem into a single, homogenized cluster—I grew up in a house surrounded by weeping willow trees. The term "waste" still triggers not-so-pleasant memories of boots, shovels and buckets, and a deep desire to run away, run away, run away.

3. **Non-Value-Adding Activity.** Using the term "non-value-adding" is a genuine problem for me. For far too many years in the 1980s, I would discuss the concept of non-value-adding activity to a room full of inspectors, expediters, rework operators, material handlers, and the like—as well as their supervisors and managers.

   Although I would explain clearly the importance of identifying all non-value-adding activities (NVA), at the end of the day most people in the room, in effect, thought I meant they were non-value-adding. That was the moment I lost them as potential participants in minimizing or even eliminating NVA.

   Although their bodies continued to show up for subsequent sessions, the hearts, minds, and hopes of these fine individuals remained permanently outside the room. They refused to identify with the NVA problem; therefore, it was impossible to get them seriously involved in solving it.

Getting individuals to I-dentify behaviors as their own is the first massive step in getting these same people to own the problems triggered by those very behaviors. In this case of the pursuit of workplace visuality, when that level of self-identification occurs, the chances rise exponentially that these very same people will want to get involved in erasing those behaviors by removing the source of motion—information deficits.

Why throw this all away to parade around expert language that may well alienate the very people whom you are trying to win over? That is one of the main reasons I have adopted the term *motion* to refer to the enemy.

But we have several more building blocks to understand before we truly appreciate the role of motion in driving workplace visuality.

Building Block 6: Work

We cannot adopt the definition of motion as moving without working without also specifying what is meant by "working," for without that detail the definition of motion is ambiguous and incomplete.

Working means *moving and adding value*. That is, we must move in order to add value, in order to work. Value does not get added by magic. This isn't the Starship Enterprise where Captain Jean-Luc Picard simply speaks into the Replicator and instantly gets a cup of "Earl Grey tea, hot!", Wedgwood china and all. In our world, we must move in order to create—in order to add value. We have to move our muscles and engage the material world in order to build a sub-assembly, grind a housing, load the cable, check a part, administer a medication or produce a proposal.

We must move in order to add value. We must work.

Work is the polar opposite of motion. If work is *moving and adding value*, then motion can be defined as *moving and not adding value*. Motion becomes anything we are compelled to do or we could not do our work.

Building Block 7: Value Field

When and where do people add value? When—and only when—they are in their *Value Field*. Their value field is where they add value. It's as simple as that. A person's value field is a specific location. It is where work happens.

This, the seventh building block of visual thinking, is a remarkable aide in helping people use motion as a diagnostic. The same crisp logic dictates that when a person is not in his/her value field, they are not working—because they are not in a location where they can add value. They are somewhere else. *They are in motion.*

Conversely, when people are in motion, they are moving without working and therefore they cannot be in their value field.

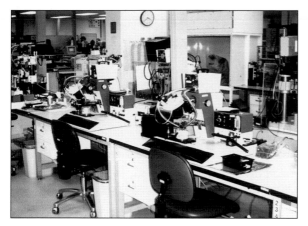

PHOTO 2.1: BONDING DEPARTMENT BEFORE (SKYWORKS SOLUTIONS, WOBURN, MA)

Naming the Value Field

Realizing where one's value field actually lies is an emerging recognition. At first, people tend to think of their departments as their value fields, and they measure their motion in relationship to that. Over time, however, this notion gets redefined as people begin to notice their motion in detail.

My favorite story of how the location of one's primary value field is redefined over time happened in the mid-1990s at Skyworks Solutions Inc.,[4] a Boston-area semi-conductor plant. I was working with a team of a dozen associates and their supervisor to roll out a demonstration cell for workplace visuality (called a *visual showcase*). The department in question was responsible for a wafer bonding process; electronic microscopes were an important operational tool. (See Photo 2.1 for what the Bonding Department looked like before workplace visuality.)

As the team moved through the steps of visual order (further explained in Chapter 5) and began to notice their motion, we asked: "Where is your value field?" To a person, the group responded: "This department, Bonding." Accordingly, people began to notice their motion—all the times that they left their value field (the Bonding Department) in order to be able to continue to work. They kept track of these times and of the reasons they had to leave; they tracked cause.

The causes were many and, for the time being, perfectly understandable:

- Looking for parts
- Getting a missing tool

- Going to get a work order clarified

- Washing off parts in a vented sink in a neighboring work area, and so on

Next, people began to bring as many of these activities as they could inside their value field (inside Bonding). They succeeded in every case but one: They still had to leave the department to wash parts in the vented sink in another area.

Once all but that cause was resituated inside the work area, the question of value field was again discussed, only this time Bernice Santos, a bonding specialist, commented: "I've been thinking. I'm not certain my real value field is this department. I think it might be my workbench. That's really where I add value." Nods all around.

BINGO! The group had its next step: Track all the times you had to leave your workbench—the newly-defined value field; track the reasons or causes and then see how many of these causes could get visually installed on or near that work station, that value field. The Bonding group did an excellent job (See photos in Photo Album 5.)

A few weeks later, we reconvened and saw that these tasks were done, splendidly. To the question, "Are we done? Has all workbench related motion been eliminated?" came nods. "Shall we check by videotape?" A few minutes later, a video camera was set up, directed at Paulette Benedictus, a veteran bonder who had volunteered to be the subject of the video (Photo 2.2). The tape would reveal whether all motion had been eliminated—or not.

Later that day, the full team gathered and watched the video. All eyes in that darkened room were on the screen, looking to see if Paulette would leave her value field, her bench—if she would engage in motion.

As we watched the tape, suddenly something truly remarkable happened—so remarkable that the entire group gasped in unison, loudly. We gasped because we had all seen the same thing, at the same moment. What did we see? This:

1. Paulette peering into her microscope, working

2. Paulette reaching for a Q-tip

3. Paulette unable to reach the Q-tip

4. Paulette looking up—GASP!

We had all seen Paulette in motion. Suddenly, motion was no longer leaving the department. Motion was not even leaving the workbench. Suddenly motion had become looking up. That's right. In a single moment in that darkened room, 14 pairs of eyes trained on the screen, every single person understood what they had not known before:

> *That the real value field in the Bonding Department was the postage-stamp size square platform at the base of the microscope.*

All motion had to be measured from there.[5]

PHOTO 2.2:
PAULETTE BENEDICTUS

Building Block 8: Motion Metrics

The final of our eight building blocks is *Motion Metrics* (the term "metric" is identical to the term "measure."). A motion metric is a mechanism or yardstick that a person uses to track or measure his/her motion. Each person tracks his/her own motion—and no one else's—typically using one or more of the following tools: stop watch, pedometer, and/or frequency check sheet.

When individuals track their own motion, they each get rock-solid data that bear witness to the struggle in a pre-visual workplace. A cable assembler at Harris Corp. watched her pedometer rack up 5.5 miles in walking in a week, without her ever leaving the department. Her colleague, who was confined to a wheelchair, used a frequency check sheet that showed she left her value field 42 times in three days. She said she had never before thought about that as a problem.

Down the aisle, in Final Test, a 27-year veteran operator saw his stopwatch record 2 hours and 35 minutes of time he spent outside his cell during a single shift. "No wonder I can't get any work done," he flashed. The supervisor of the area simply kept track of all the questions she asked and was asked, and soon understood her own motion and what was eating up all her time.[6]

Motion metrics give people a concrete way to demonstrate to themselves why they cannot get a full day of work done.

The beauty part of measuring motion is that it can be done so simply and can motivate such high levels of ownership. The key is to make sure to let people measure their own motion. This is crucial. It is not just unnecessary for a supervisor or technician to track another person's motion, it is counterproductive, working against the very outcomes that motion metrics are designed to generate.

One of the greatest challenges of any improvement initiative is to get people on board. In this day and age, nearly everything seems elective, with many individuals expressing a tremendous sense of entitlement and prerogative over the simplest choices. Some simply refuse to cooperate. You may call it resistance, but they see it as their right. If you are a manager or supervisor, you may be tempted to threaten those who will not get on board. Not only does that no longer work, doing so will almost always kill an improvement activity because others are watching.

We discuss this matter at length in the next two chapters; in fact, it is their entire focus.

Asking people to track their own motion (to collect their own motion metrics) cuts through the cultural miasma that many enterprises have created. From there, creating visual devices is only a step away, and with them, all the attendant benefits of a highly competent visual workplace.

Putting It All Together

You have just learned about the eight building blocks of visual thinking. Now let's look at how they work together to help the workforce eliminate motion and the information deficits that cause it by inventing visual solutions. It is called the *Cycle of Visual Thinking* (Figure 2.7).

The first step in this cycle is for us to notice our motion.

Step 1: Notice the motion.

Look! I just left my value field. That means I'm not working anymore. I must be in motion.

Step 2: Name the information deficit.

Hmmm, if I am in motion, there must be an information deficit—a missing answer. What is it?

Step 3: Ask the un-answered core question.

Which of the six core questions needs to be answered?

Step 4: Decide where to physically install the missing answer so it is right at hand.

How close can I get the answer to the actual point of use?

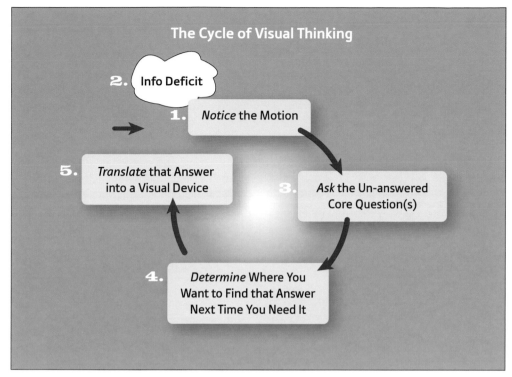

FIGURE 2.7: THE CYCLE OF VISUAL THINKING

Step 5: Translate that answer into a visual device.

> Now I'll turn that answer into a visual solution—and I won't ever have to ask or answer that question again because the answer will be firmly installed as close to the point-of-use as possible.

Excellent! Now at the least sign of more motion, the visual thinker starts the cycle again.

Person after person, cycle after cycle, this is exactly how the people who work in your company (on each organizational level) populate the work environment with dozens, hundreds, even thousands, of visual devices and mini-systems that result in an enterprise of splendid visual transparency.

Photo Album 5

Making the Value Field Visual

Visually Ordering the Value Fields

Under the improvement leadership of Kenny Bushmich and Annie Yu, workplace visuality at Skyworks Solutions* (Boston) turned the company into one of the best visual facilities in New England. This album shows the *visual where* on the benches of the Bonding Department and nearby areas.

Note: Because of anti-static process requirements, the red ESD** tape seen here was used for work surfaces borders; regular plastic tape was used on floors.

◀ The simple metal tray on the left of the value field is for small work implements, placed on a slant to ease pick/put. Each of the tray's small compartments has a photo-copied border taped to the bottom, doing double-duty as the address for what resides there. ▼

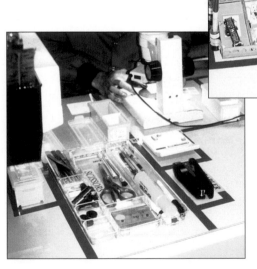

◀ A plastic tray bought at the local office supply store provides another excellent storage space for small work items. The address for each compartment is under the thing that resides there.

*Formerly Alpha Industries   **Electric Static Discharge

Visual is in the Details

Skyworks implemented visual order thoroughly, especially on work surfaces, putting many key visual details in place for the benefit of the company and individual associates.

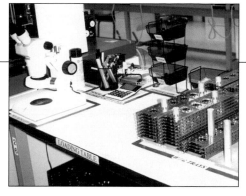

Research shows that bold black letters on a crayon-yellow background are the most readable color combination. We see this applied throughout Skyworks. ➟ ▶

Doors (and drawers) are automatic motion-makers because they require us to do something (open them) before we can get to what we really want. Visual workplace practices tell us to get rid of as many doors (and drawers) as possible. But when a process requires doors, as this one at Skyworks does, consider using plastic or Plexiglas. ▶

Chapter 2 Footnotes

1. Hank's story is mentioned in passing in my first book on workplace visuality, *Visual Systems: Harnessing the Power of a Visual Workplace*, page 9.

2. More about the *visual where* in Chapter 5.

3. The old and moldy "4Ws+2Hs." Finally, they make sense.

4. Formerly Alpha Industries.

5. Now, fully ten years later, re-telling this incident still gives me goose bumps.

6. And then of course, she applied the First-Question-Is-Free Rule and populated the area with supervisory-level visual solutions that shared vital information and served everyone.

Section | Two

THE CULTURE CONVERSION

How change gets implemented is precisely as important as what that change is. The most successful transformations are a perfect blending of the two—a perfect blending of the How and What, the two wings of a bird as discussed in Chapter 1.

As will become increasingly clear in a later section of this book, the technologies of the visual workplace represent a proven protocol, a strategy, for imbedding informational transparency into the enterprise, on all levels—from maintenance to the executive board room, from the shop floor to engineering, from quality to finance. The result is enterprise-wide visuality.

Yet a successful and sustainable implementation of any kind cannot be dropped down into an existing work culture as a pre-built framework, imposed on associates from outside. However beautiful and elegant that improvement framework might be, by itself it will not thrive. Models and frameworks are nothing without people to drive them—people with all of their vision, strength, and skill as well as their baggage of disappointments, bad habits, and fear of change.

So before we can even consider "yet another improvement scheme," we must understand the people-level of the workplace—the work culture of the organization.

The two chapters in this section address the cultural dimension of a company's journey to excellence. Early in the process of implementing workplace visuality, this dimension is engaged and amplified. It happens first as the *visual where* is installed. Here at the outset of the journey, the enterprise has a unique opportunity to create a work culture aligned with continuous improvement, if one is not yet in place—or to strengthen it if it already is.

While the technical details of implementing the *visual where* come in a later chapter, Chapter 3 shows us that logic from the perspective of the company's executive leadership, and Chapter 4 looks at this from the vantage point of the value-add employee.

Nothing changes if nothing changes.
Hindu Proverb

C H A P T E R | **3**

Leadership and the Power Inversion

A company's work culture is that combination of corporate purpose, beliefs, values, expectations, and behaviors that define and reflect what winning means in the organization and how the game is played.

Work culture has the power to inspire or dishearten. It can be as powerful in the absence of a coherent set of corporate purpose, beliefs, values, expectations, and behaviors as it is when these are fully in place. In fact, in many companies, work culture is more of an accident than a clear intent.

It doesn't have to be that way. An effective implementation of workplace visuality can and has resuscitated a gloomy, dis-spirited workforce and turned it into one that can be described as spirited, engaged, contributing, creative—and aligned. Aligned with what? Aligned with the corporate intent.

When we implement the technologies of the visual workplace, we don't just change the physical operational environment and accelerate the flow of material, information, and people in and through the facility. We align the work culture with the improvement vision of the enterprise. In some cases, we completely recast that culture, giving it a new set of premises, requirements, and goals. It is transformed.

This chapter will treat this shift in culture shift from the ancient end of the continuum, where much has to change and a great deal more simply has to be eliminated from the mind and heart of the organization. We call the kind of culture that needs a full overhaul, *traditional,* and its opposite—a unified and aligned work culture—*new.*[1]

The Challenge: Need for a New Paradigm

The vast majority of organizations around this country and around the world are just beginning their journey to excellence. Such companies are faced with a mighty challenge: They not only have to reverse their production values (adopting batch-size-of-one in lieu of large batches; designing layouts based on flow instead of function; building quality *in* instead of inspecting it *out*), they also have to rethink and reformulate the habits, assumptions, and preferences of nearly every member of the workforce, including those of management itself.

Most companies do not grasp the scope and scale of the change that is required when they first consider altering the conventions of their production process. After all, they say, changing lot size is challenge enough. How could there be more? Yet there is more, a great deal more. That "more" may be set to the side for a time, but it cannot be ignored.

The fabric of a work culture is the sum total of each and every interaction and data point that transpires within a given shift, day, week, month, and year—for the life of the company. Work culture is not an isolated event. It exists across the life of the company, and it expresses the quality of that work life. It is the context of production; it is the context of performance.

In a manner of speaking, work culture represents the personality as well as the consciousness of the enterprise. It mirrors its soul.[2] Work culture describes, explains, and defines who the enterprise is, what it is about, what it values, and, accordingly, how it conducts itself. All of that is available for the world to see. The company is its work culture.

Every part that is made, every deadline met or missed, every piece of information shared or lost, every truth, every lie, every promise made or broken, impacts the culture of work and re-shapes it, however minutely. No detail is immune. The conversion of the production system to lean—the installation of a pull system and an accelerated flow—requires a parallel and intentional transformation in the work culture. Changing your production approach will certainly impact the culture of work in your organization; but it will not align your culture sufficiently to raise that impact to a level of sustainable excellence.

Even companies with well-oiled paternalistic frameworks of governance must change. The genie is out of the bottle. If you had to land on one word that captured the substance of that change, that word would be *empowerment*. This revolution in consciousness was triggered fifty years ago, and the world is still unraveling its implications and applications. In business and industry, much of that activity is trained on the conversion of the work culture into one of greater balance and greater power. We seek a new paradigm of *governance*, a new way to define and distribute power.

The Big Picture: The Two Pyramids of Power

The old paradigm has many names: the top-down pyramid, command and control approach, the military model, paternalist governance or my own personal favorite— The Thumb (Figure 3.1).

Whatever its name, obedience is at its heart. *I say and you do. I order and you obey. I know and you don't.*

In the top-down model, the general, CEO or manager sits at the top of the heap, at the apex of the pyramid—and the foot soldiers (line employees/operators/value-add associates)—line the base. Command and control is the way fathers raised their children at the turn-of-the-century (and before). Three generations later, that was how my Swiss-born father raised me—with a heavy hand and zero tolerance for my opinion. It was a very popular model at the time, widely accepted as the only way: the Boss (or Pop) at the top of the heap; the child (*moi*) at the bottom. Thus was the tree bent.

From many perspectives, this approach was an undisputed success. It helped industrialize nations, win wars, and colonize the world. Rules, regulations, protocols, requirements, standards, decorum, structure—in the U.S., these were the forces that helped pull a disparate population of immigrants into a thriving economy. Who would argue with that? This was the approach that got things done; and

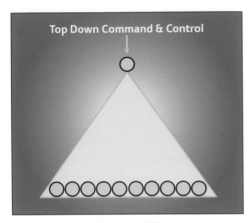

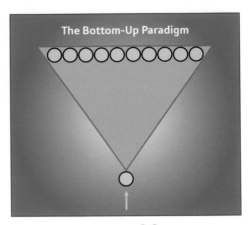

FIGURE 3.2:
THE TOP-DOWN PARADIGM

FIGURE 3.3:
THE BOTTOM-UP PARADIGM

they stayed done. It was the paradigm of task.

If personal preferences or independent thinking took a back seat to orders from the boss, it was a small sacrifice to pay for stability, predictability, and control. Only recently have we discovered that the top-down model is out of balance; and we discovered why: It represents only half of the equation. There is another half—and it is the mirror opposite of the paternalistic approach. (What did we know?)

The name of that opposite is the bottom-up model (Figure 3.3). The foot soldiers now line the uppermost edge of the pyramid (previously the base), with the general/commandeer/CEO occupying the bottom (formerly the apex). The notion of leadership is literally turned on its head. The supreme commander now becomes the servant-leader.[3] And whom does that leader serve? The value-add associate; the hourly employee.

The message is clear: The leader's role in this new paradigm is to help value-add associates become more effective in their work and more engaged. He is servant-leader; as such, he attunes and listens to the needs of those whom he serves. This is his job.

The bottom-up pyramid represents the empowerment model. Its goal is greater participation, greater employee effectiveness, and the sharing of power. Because the pyramid is inverted, the power and authority of the enterprise flows upwards into the line of value. The focus of leadership has shifted to promoting and tangibly supporting others so that process, flow, quality, safety, and cost improve (that's long-hand for the improvement of overall lead time). The emphasis is not on the leader accomplishing his tasks but on his helping others accomplish theirs.

For the value-add associate, the focus is no longer on unquestioning obedience. The focus is now on line employees studying and understanding the process, not obeying the rules. Line employees are asked to become masters of cause and scientists of their own process.

False Decision-Point: Which One to Choose?

The bottom-up paradigm is the polar opposite of the top-down model, inverted as it is with all previous assumptions, preferences, principles, and values upside down. In this inversion, the previous power structure seems erased. But that is not so. Any attempt to remove the previous power base (the top-down approach) would almost certainly destroy the entire organization, not just the executive level.

Yet, in the early 1980s, such attempts were made, however wrongly, when we first began to learn about empowerment and its value. Back then, companies suddenly understood the immense power in harnessing the minds and hearts—and not just the hands and feet—of the workforce. They rushed headlong into that; and, in their haste, some companies mistakenly dismantled their executive or middle management structure.

In wholly replacing the top-down paradigm with that of the bottom-up, those companies erroneously turned over the running of their companies to quality circles and other empowerment configurations. They were surprised when the enterprise failed—but you and I, with the benefit of hindsight, are not. We see now that they threw the baby out with the bathwater.

Two Pyramids: Two Functions

In the top-down paradigm, the executive is responsible for vision, mission, values, strategy, systems, and structure. His/her position at the top of the pyramid provides the long view that allows the corporation to align with its long-term objectives. The CEO sets the framework in place, answering the "what," "why," and "who":

1. What are we about? What are our products and services? What is our common purpose? What are our strategic objectives?

2. Why is any of the above important? Why bother?

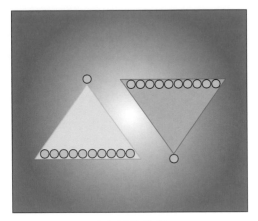

FIGURE 3.4:
DIFFERENT FUNCTION—
DIFFERENT GROUPS

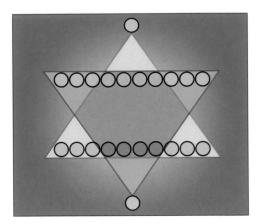

FIGURE 3.5:
THE RESOLUTION
OF OPPOSITES

3. Who is responsible for these "whats" and "whys"?

The so-called "head of the snake" is responsible for defining and executing these tasks.

By contrast, the bottom-up pyramid focuses on the "how"—how the purpose is deployed; how the objectives are meant to be met; how products and services are to be made and delivered; and how Operations is used to fulfill the corporate intent. In terms of the value-add level, the empowerment approach asks employees to become scientists of their own process on a local level and to find ways to improve and upgrade that process, systematically and continuously.

These are two very different functions, executed by two distinct groups (Figure 3.5). In the face of such dramatic opposites, some companies struggle to decide which of the two pyramids to embrace and which to erase. These are the wrong questions.

We cannot throw either approach out. Instead, we must resolve or blend these two seeming opposites into a single paradigm. Why? Because the enterprise needs both of them.

If Figure 3.6 looks familiar to you, it is because it is an ancient symbol that has been used by many of the world's civilizations and religions since time immemorial.[4] In its original ancient depictions, this image of two triangles is always inscribed in a circle (the two triangles are actually pyramids or tetrahedrons, and the circle a sphere). From ancient times, a star tetrahedron inscribed in a sphere has been a universal symbol for unity.

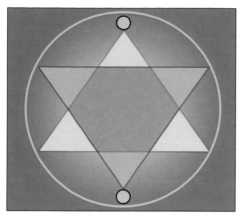

FIGURE 3.6:
ANCIENT SYMBOL
OF UNITY

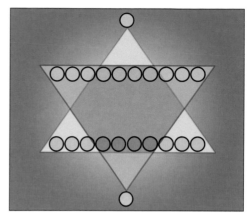

FIGURE 3.7:
THE GEOGRAPHY OF
COMMON GROUND

Think about it. Choose any set of opposites: blacks and whites, us and them, male and female, Muslims and Jews, Pro-Choice and Pro-Life, Democrats and Republicans, managers and hourly employees. How do these extremes find resolution? How can they become unified? There is only one way: They must look for common ground. The work of unification is finding that common ground.

Creating a blend of these is not just hard work. It is transformative. When they do combine, notice what happens to polar opposites (Figure 3.7). Only a portion of Figure 3.7 is perfectly blended: The green section in the center. This green area is the geography of common ground. Around it remain sections of different-ness, exclusive and distinct. Pure yellow. Pure blue. Unaffected one by the other.

Committed to finding common ground? You are in for some hard work—and tremendous reward.

Let me illustrate with a story.

Pro-Life and Pro-Choice Come to an Agreement

It's hard to find more polar opposites than the Pro-Life and Pro-Choice movements in the U.S. Each has an iron-clad set of values and premises that supports its own correctness and brooks no argument.

So it was quite a surprise when the two groups in a small Midwestern city began talking to each other back in the mid-1980s. One said to the other, "Listen, we are each so convinced of our own rightness and the other's wrongness that one of these days we might start killing each other. Why don't we sit down and try to understand each other (even though we know we can never ever agree) so we don't further polarize."

The two groups decided to meet once a week and take turns in explaining their own perspective. One group would present; the other would listen.

They engaged in this under an unusual ground rule: the listening group would not begin stating its position until the presenting group had said everything it wanted to say and determined that the listening group had understood. Both groups agreed to the following definition of the term "understood": When the listening group could repeat back the position and perspective of the presenting group to the presenting group's satisfaction, it would be taken that the listening group had understood.

With that, a coin was tossed at the first meeting to determine which group would begin. Pro-Life won. Pro-Life began to explain its beliefs, values, and premises; and, at every step of the way, Pro-Choice was obliged to repeat back its understanding of what was said until Pro-Life said, "Yes, now you understand."

That part of the process took nearly six months. When it was complete, the roles were reversed. Pro-Choice spoke; and Pro-Life listened and sought to comprehend and appreciate until it could repeat back the Pro-Choice party line to the satisfaction of the Pro-Choice group. That took another six months.

At the end of a year, the two groups—polar opposites—understood the other group's position, even though they still did not agree with it, not one bit.

In the wisdom of the moment, the two groups then decided that they did not want to throw the opportunity away. They decided to search for common ground—some area of endeavor they could enter into together. After yet more discussion, they realized that they both had an abiding interest in the welfare of children. They began to meet once a month to work together on children's projects.

Though the two groups kept their differences and held to these fiercely, they had found common ground (the green center) and arrived at enough agreement for them to move forward together (at least, on an issue of mutual interest).

Finding common ground (areas of overlap between two opposites) requires that we pursue consensus, defined as: *The active search for disagreement until enough agreement is met for us to move forward together.* We learn a new way.

The Business Connection

That is exactly what is transpiring in companies throughout this country and around the world. Executives and senior managers are learning a new way. Hourly employees are learning a new way. Neither is easy. Both groups are indispensable to the running of the company. Each is powerful.

When we talk about transforming the work culture, we are talking about this process, which is, at its foundation, a balancing of power. The roles and the power bases remain distinct. Executives and senior managers still have their own set of duties, responsibilities, and functions. Hourly employees still have theirs. There is no effort to blend these. Instead, both sides commit to identifying and embracing a common purpose—achieving enterprise excellence for the prosperity and long life of the company, shareholders, workforce, and the community-at-large. When found, this common purpose allows both sides to deploy their strengths for that common good. They seek to pool these strengths, not become homogenized.

Caught in the Middle[5]

Before we take a closer look at the mechanics of this change, we need to look at another player in the shifting of this balance: middle managers and supervisors (union leaders included).

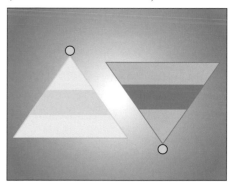

FIGURE 3.8:
CAUGHT IN THE MIDDLE

These employees are the translation point of the change, carrying messages between the apex and the base, and operationalizing the new paradigm of power/empowerment (Figure 3.8).

This is no easy task. The goals of the general and the foot soldier are clearly defined— but lieutenants and sergeants have to make them happen. Theirs is a role of support, coaching, and influence. Traditionally speaking, middle managers and supervisors are the problem-solvers of the enterprise. Most of the time, the problems are not theirs but are inherited from generals and foot soldiers, with both groups expecting solutions.

Supervisors and managers are caught in the middle in the traditional organization. They are caught in the middle in the new organization. And they are caught in the middle in the transition between the two. As you will learn in this book's third section, a specific set of visual workplace technologies is designed to help

> *Discipline is remembering what you love.* —*Albert Einstein*

them in this task and beyond. But the inversion must first be initiated.

The How of Empowerment: The Hidden Geometry

The top-down pyramid is the starting point for the process of converting the work culture (Figure 3.9). That is because companies that need to convert are, by definition, functioning from the top-down model. They could never go into business or stay in business for very long without it. Command and control is the make-decisions/get-things-done line of attack. It requires action.

Yet, when we study this form closely, we see that the top-down pyramid contains another one. Just inside the command and control pyramid is empowerment—dormant, waiting, and powerful but only in its potential. The bottom-up paradigm is imbedded, hidden, in the top-down approach; it is imprisoned there.

This hidden geometry, in effect, is both a seed and a promise. When we begin to see the shortcomings of the obedience paradigm, we understand that the way to address those shortcomings is by inverting (not subverting) its power. We turn to the workforce and in a sense say,"We still need obedience. But this time we want you to obey a deeper knowing than just the rules. We want you to find and then listen to your inner drive for excellence. Yours is a new power mandate: Become a scientist of the process. Get to know it for yourself. Get informed. Get educated. And then get active in making it better."

This variation on the theme of obedience is closely akin to the refreshing definition of discipline that Albert Einstein provides us. *Discipline*, Dr. Einstein tells us, *is remembering what you love.* Here we have culture as an outcome in a single phrase. In Einstein's rendering, *discipline* is synonymous with ownership, engagement, and alignment.

Could it be that the premier physicist of our era and *TIME* magazine's Man of the Century is proclaiming the power of love in the workplace? That is exactly the case.

When we love doing something, we do not need to be reminded, prodded, micro-managed or threatened. We simply do it. If we are blocked from doing it temporarily, we find a way around obstruction and do it anyway. Why? Because we love it. We want to get back to it. It feeds us.

The challenge in converting a traditional work culture to an improvement work culture is finding the way to ignite that sense of ownership, engagement, and alignment. After that, the care, momentum, and sustainment take care of themselves. They emerge naturally and powerfully from that base.

This is in no way to suggest that improvement becomes continuous just because people enjoy doing it. With so many priorities competing for time and resources in most companies, wanting to

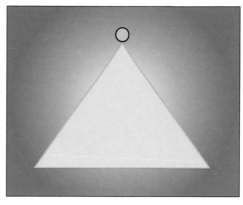

FIGURE 3.9:
THE TOP-DOWN PYRAMID
(EMPOWERMENT IS HIDDEN WITHIN IT)

do something and actually getting it done can be two different stories. As you will read, there are numerous visual tools and applications that can help us harness the drive for excellence so it can be put to work for the betterment of the corporation.

Liberating the Hidden Pyramid: A Closer Look

Transitioning into an organization that authentically reflects genuine unity is a long journey that is accomplished in no less than four courageous steps.

The first step is simply for management to notice the imbalances that the traditional authoritarian approach has created in the enterprise when that kind of strength works as the sole driver of the work culture. Step two is management's decision to define, develop, and deploy the dynamics of empowerment and make it a way of life in the company. In step three, management lays out the plan for all of the above; and, in step four, the plan is deployed.

Tipping the culture in favor of empowerment until it is on an equal footing with executive leadership can only happen gradually, nearly imperceptibly at first.

The first nearly imperceptible shift is when the inertia that holds empowerment a prisoner of the authoritarian approach breaks (Figure 3.10). The two pyramids separate. How? Since inertia is a powerful force, it requires an equally powerful force to break its hold. In workplace visuality, this moment occurs when line employees are put in charge of installing their own *visual where*. This is the compelling first step in initiating this separation (and there is much more on this

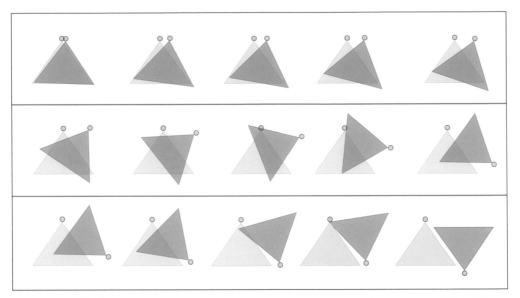

FIGURE 3.10: THE SEPARATION + INVERSION OF THE BOTTOM-UP PYRAMID

point in the next chapter).

In doing so, the iron-hold of the command and control approach is broken and the bottom-up pyramid is released, free at last to begin to invert. Slowly it will find its true orientation and distinctiveness. At the conclusion of this process, which can take many months, the two paradigms exist in parallel, side-by-side. Figure 3.10 suggests the incremental nature of this progression.

Next, as shown in Figure 3.11, begins the accommodation phase. The two separate forces (top/down and bottom/up) begin to shift towards each other again, only this time each will retain its own unique distinctiveness as it moves into balance and overlaps with the other.

The end result is unity, with a simultaneous definition of both areas of commonality and enduring differences.

Participation Myths

Remember, though I am illustrating this progression through a series of simple shapes and explaining it smoothly, the actual process drives change into the heart of the organization, where a host of formal and informal values reside. This conversion is rarely simple, smooth or quick. It is, instead, often messy, confusing, and time-intensive. But one way or the other, in our experience, the separation between

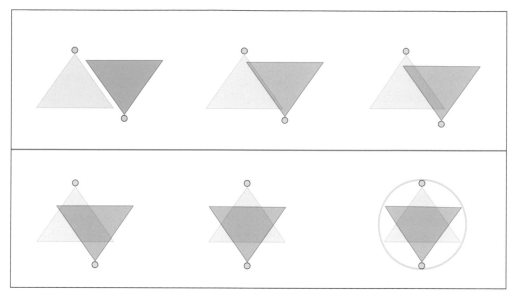

FIGURE 3.11: THE TWO MODELS APPROACH AND BLEND

the two powers, the inversion, and then the final integration, are required for companies committed to excellence.

For some, however, empowerment is such a potent dynamic that they prefer to move towards it in small doses. Typically companies that decide to take it slow do so because they fear that anarchy will result instead of unity. But they are wrong. Anarchy is nowhere to be found in this progression.

The only true danger is backsliding—backsliding into the old authoritarian paradigm; and that can only happen if the process is begun but not completed. However much a company may say it wants an empowered workforce and a balanced work culture, if management elects to proceed piecemeal, it runs the risk of diluting the very momentum it must gain if the shift is to be made. As a result, the conversion is never achieved.

To be sure, those organizations that stay the course will experience moments of discomfort as managers witness what momentarily looks like a loss of control. This seeming loss is of the very control they know that they will have to—and in fact want to—release if they are to enter the new paradigm at all.

There can be no better moment to exercise the artistry of change—but this is also the moment when the company knows the least about what to do or how to do it. Colossal mistakes can and often do get made.

Prescriptively, I will tell you that to succeed in this transformation you must designate an implementation team to oversee it—a group of skillful, experienced, emotionally sturdy individuals who will remain alert to predictable pitfalls.[6]

There are many methods for successfully converting the work culture. No single method is sufficient to induce, produce, and then sustain the entire change. Yet, in my experience, an effective implementation of the technologies of the visual workplace comes the closest in creating this outcome.[7]

In workplace visuality, we call that outcome: creating a workforce of visual thinkers. In my view, this is a new world-class competency that is capable of shifting the enterprise into balance and unity, and catapulting it into outrageous profit margins. It is the most effective way we have found for both liberating the individual will that is currently imbedded in the obedience paradigm and getting the bottom-up pyramid to disengage and begin its inversion.

Employee involvement does not surface easily or naturally on its own, especially in a company accustomed to the rule of command and control. Often the real legacy of an organization rooted in the top-down/obedience approach is arrogance and abuse of power on the leadership side, and ballistic anger or numbness on the value-add side. Both breed a deep sense of helplessness and entrenched passivity.

In such organizations, managers often complain that the workforce does not want empowerment, remembering the many times they have offered hourly employees opportunities to participate and were refused. When the time came, line employees either sneered or said nothing; they simply sat there even when, protests management, a great deal of what was meaningful to them was at stake.

Yes, some line employees may give it a half-hearted try—or two. But then in the face of the usual "no extra time provided for improvement,"[8] associates wisely write employee involvement off as another empty promise. Not long after that, managers may also write off employee involvement—because employees do not appear interested in responding, even when given a "special invitation."

In the face of this seeming belligerence and/or indifference, managers mistakenly conclude that the workforce does not want participation, or does not appreciate participation, or does not want to be bothered. "These people don't care! They're just plain lazy," managers conclude.

What they overlook is the truth: *The workforce does not know how to participate.* It is a mystery. They don't know what this new kind of employee involvement could mean since, to them, they have always been involved in what, up to now, management has said is important—producing, doing work, adding value, showing up. The only participation they know is the work itself. That's how they have been asked to participate, year-after-year, job-after-job: "Just do your work." And they do.

And now management is asking them to do yet more. How can such an undertaking possibly succeed?

Because most managers have experienced what I just described more than once in their careers, they tend to skip right over the "special invitation" part and go directly to one of their two favorite forms of improvement participation:

1. Doing the improvement themselves and/or with their peers; or

2. Handpicking the best of the lot from the ranks and assigning these "high-achievers" a role in an event-based improvement activity such as a Kaizen Blitz, Special SWAT Team or the like.

I do not mean to suggest that handpicking members for your improvement teams is not a useful option, especially for event-based improvement efforts. It may be exactly right for your purposes. It is, however, not the most effective way to align and unify the enterprise. It certainly is not the most effective or efficient way to create an empowered workforce.

None of these scenarios (managers doing it themselves, writing off the possibility of empowerment because "people are lazy anyway," or handpicking the implementers) will advance the inversion of the hidden pyramid. You need radical new vision and the courage to deploy it. That vision must be rooted in the values of the change you say you want. In that way, you know how to respond when the unusual or unforeseen occurs.

The fact is companies in transition from a traditional to a new enterprise often do not know how to create a true participation-based organization. They do not know how to structure in the opportunity for people to routinely and reliably contribute their ideas locally—on behalf of the greater corporate intent. Yet just because the company has not yet learned how to do this does not mean that the possibility does not exist—or that employees will always either not have any ideas to contribute or simply refuse to contribute them.

Thinking so is a problem in itself because, in all cases, such a mindset brings us to the wrong conclusions and closes the door on solutions that are genuinely available.

Nonetheless, one must realize that mistakes made at the earliest phase of this journey are the most difficult to correct, no less so when implementing workplace visuality as anything else. The Chinese proverb "the first step of the journey is the destination" applies here.

The Biggest Mistake

There are no less than ten doorways into workplace visuality.[9] Each doorway leads to a distinct category of visual function (visual order, visual standards, visual metrics, visual displays, and so on). Each doorway is opened by a different organizational group or mix of groups—each responsible for imbedding a specific visual outcome into the corporate landscape. Line employees, managers, engineers, maintenance personnel, quality technicians, supervisors, executives, and support staff each make a special contribution.

Implementing automatic recoil (the *visual where*) is the doorway reserved for employees on the value-add level, whatever the setting—factory, hospital, insurance office, home delivery vehicle, or retail store. This task is reserved for them.

The formula is simple: a border, home address, and (if possible) an ID label for everything that casts a shadow. No exception. This lays down the pattern of work and installs automatic recoil—the ability of a workplace item to find its way back home, based solely on the visual location information built into it.

Time and again, an effective implementation of the *visual where* produces a 15% to 30% increase in throughput on the cell or departmental level, with parallel reductions in flow distance and lead time, as well as dramatic improvements in quality and on-time delivery. It also serves as the single trigger to the mighty work culture conversion we have just discussed—the release and then inversion of the empowerment pyramid.

But such outcomes require that managers not take short cuts—though they will be tempted.

The first mistake that management can make is exactly here, at the launch of visual order. Because this pitfall comes at the very outset of the visual conversion, it can easily become the company's biggest implementation mistake. What is that mistake? Management appropriates the simple chore of installing the *visual where* for itself, assigns it only to a few hand-picked associates or delegates it to some group other than line employees.

Yes, the most fundamental error managers can make at the earliest stage of a rich and productive transformation is to commandeer the simple task of implementing the *visual where* for themselves. Such managers mean no harm. They reason only that, because the task is so simple and obvious, they can do it themselves (or contract it out) and save operators for more interesting improvement tasks. "Lines, labels, addresses! That's easy."

But they are mistaken. The very simplicity of installing the *visual where* is one of the main reasons why it can move the company into and through the inversion experience.

The Visual Where: Low-Hanging Fruit

Installing the *visual where* is like picking so much low-hanging fruit. When managers decide to pick that fruit themselves, they unintentionally rob the organization of a prime opportunity to *empower the value-add level workforce*.

It is just because installing the *visual where* is so elementary—and yet so useful to day-to-day performance—that operators should be the ones to implement it. Operators decide. Operators design. Operators explore. Operators experiment. Operators invent.[10] You can only engender an empowered workforce if you provide the workforce with powerful tasks to undertake. This is at the heart of the I-driven approach.

In implementing visual order, we ask the most valuable group in the enterprise—value-add associates—to help to improve their own work area and their own work flow by getting the workplace to speak the answer to the *where* question again and again. The dialogue is between the employee and his/her own work. Having line employees install the *visual where* is a vital component in the company getting the workforce to connect to the physicality of the change.

We let the experts pick that fruit. This is genuine empowerment, providing the company with a new core competency that prepares it for the other transformative changes that must happen if the company is to achieve excellence.

In this first phase of the journey, employees find and follow their own internal improvement vision—every employee. This is the heart of the I-driven paradigm. Each person is asked to be in charge of his or her own locus of control and use the need-to-know as a stimulus to populate that local real estate with visual devices and mini-systems that answer that need.

You can think of I-driven as self-motivated (as in "I can"). It can also easily

FIGURE 3.12: THE NEED-TO-KNOW

embrace the concepts of Inventiveness ("I will") and Inspiration ("I want."). You get the picture.

There is no way to over-emphasize the importance of the I-driven dynamic in creating and sustaining workplace visuality. Indeed, I-driven will continue as a theme again and again in the chapters of this book; and maybe after all that, I will have succeeded in making the beginnings of a case for its importance. Just maybe.

When we aim to establish a new way of thinking in the enterprise—visual thinking—we deliberately look for ways to make each person independent and singular in his or her actions, in his or her own improvement ideas. Let me repeat: To many, this seems counter-intuitive, the antithesis of creating a unified, team-based work culture. It is, in fact, a strong step in precisely the right direction. (See the case study on the next page.)

This I-driven process, which is primarily designed to engage and empower the value-add employee, is the subject of the next chapter.

A VISUAL TRUCK MINI-CASE STUDY

SEARS HOME REPAIR TRUCKS

ANGIE ALVARADO

FRANK LOPUSZYNSKI

DISTRICT 8368

- 337 Trucks
- 301 Technicians
- 421 Total Associates
- Total Area: half of California and Nevada
- An average of seven home visits per technician per day
- 376,574 Home visits in 2003
- 404,023 Home visits in 2004

Angie Alvarado: In Her Own Words
INVERTING THE PYRAMID

When Sears Home Services (Illinois) decided to launch visual order in its Product Repair Services division, the goal was to shave minutes off of each home visit that 8,400 repair technicians made daily. The focus was the repair truck.

Each repair truck is akin to an entire department—everything the technician needs to make a repair is in it: parts, tools, manuals, the computer that linked to Sears home base, and so on. The truck is the technician's life line.

Under the leadership of Frank Lopuszynski, divisional Director of Operations, District 8368 became the pilot for a visual truck rollout at the Sacramento (CA) Center. Angie Alvarado started as a phone sales rep at Sears 18 years ago and has been General Manager of District 8368 for eight years. Sacramento is her home base.

THE SACRAMENTO CENTER

Productivity—more work with less payroll—is a major goal in all companies, and we at Sears Parts & Repair Services (Sacramento, CA) are no exception. One of our main productivity metrics revolves around technician repair times: how much time a technician actually spends in a customer's home, repairing appliances. Decreasing repair times had always been a goal. We talked about it daily, and our goals and recognition programs all circled around it. But our search to improve repair time without sacrificing repair quality found no answers.

⬆ **Before:** Trucks got pretty darn cluttered. Legend has it that one tech, in need of a screw, decided it would be quicker to take it off the truck body itself than to try to find it under all that jumble.

Three years ago, my boss asked if I had ever heard of 5S, because he needed a volunteer for a project. I had a book about 5S on my shelf, so I signed on, even though I was a little insulted. After all, I had the cleanest and most organized facility in the Western Region.

Three months later, Dr. G (Gwendolyn Galsworth) walked in with her crew of visual worker bees. We toured the facility together. I introduced her to some technicians and proudly announced our success on metric after metric. Dr. G listened, took time to ask for clarification, and praised us on our successes.

Dr. G and I spent the next year together. I learned that while 5S may start with being clean and organized, the *visual workplace* engages your employees to share information and make it readily accessible to others. Employees are assigned improvement time to improve their work space and (oh, yes) increase productivity.

Productivity—that brings us back to the repair time question. Well, the answer was there all along and it was not in training or more and better tools. The answer was in the workspace, the value field—the repair truck itself. The technician spends most of his day in the truck—driving to the customer's home, going back to the truck to locate a tool, and then one more time (we hope only one more time) to find a needed part.

So, was the answer to clean and organize the truck, as in "Let's have a Kaizen event and clean all the trucks"? No. Some of our techs had very clean and organized trucks (like our facility) and yet their repair times and productivity were no higher than anyone else's. The issue was visuality—all the neat, clean, and organized parts, for example, in near-identical little brown boxes with small labels and even smaller part numbers. The technicians could not tell the differ-

▲ **After:** Everything is accessible, clear, safe, and visually ordered. This tech even decided to carpet the floor of her truck!

This cab speaks for itself! ▲

THE VISUAL TRUCK

◀ The tech on this truck lists parts on these pink cards, crossing them out as consumed.

Each appliance manual on this truck is visually ordered. ▼

ence, so they decided to address the racks that held the parts. Smart move. Very visual.

Technicians stopped fighting with their workspace and embraced it as their own. That's right. We did not dictate a standardized workspace. Instead, we asked each technician to decide what worked best for him/her. We wanted them to come up with new ways. Some technicians labeled the racks with pictures of the parts; others made binders with diagrams of the truck interior. Most used color coding.

Visually ordered, color-coded bins with bold addresses helped a lot. ▼

My team and I set a course to embrace this new and exciting concept. The technicians came into the facility with their trucks once a month to show off their new visual ideas to management and each other. We kept lots of supplies on hand in the Visual Corner so techs could run with any improvement idea they had—bins, baskets, tape, pre-cut pegboard panels, Velcro, hooks, and more. We developed recognition programs around this monthly event.

ONE OF THE TWO TECH GROUPS IN THE VISUAL PILOT.

When your entire "department" is a truck, space is at a premium. The Sears techs applied S4/Select Locations principles (smart placement) to their new blue trucks—especially the one that instructs us to store things, not air. Take a look.

⬆ The precut pegboard panels from the Visual Corner gave techs lots of ideas on how to visually use the dead space on the back doors.

These visually ordered parts bins were mounted on a wooden frame and do more than you think. See the latch? Open it and the frame swings forward to the point of use—while also allowing the tech to access the shelves behind it. Close it and the items on those shelves stay safely in place. ⬇

Techs also made great use of the dead space tucked up in the corner where doors open. ⬇

We set criteria for visual concepts and gave cash awards to the best "visual truck".

Employee morale soared. Oh, and yes, productivity improved, too—15% across the board.

Trust was another unexpected result. Before visuality, we locked up pens and other supplies—because we were certain that people would steal them. As a result, all managers had to have a ton of keys or know somebody who did.

We don't do that anymore. All supplies are in their addressed locations, open to anyone who needs them. Supplies don't disappear. Employees don't hoard. And the company doesn't spend money on endless replenishments. People know where things are and they use what they need.

Repair time? Well, that measurement never improved—yet customer satisfaction, quality repair scores, and revenue all increased. Yes, the technicians were spending less time in their trucks looking for parts and tools and more time (saved time) with customers—listening, getting better information about the needed repair, and offering to fix other appliances.

Revenues went up by $1.5 million in a year. Customer satisfaction (which at Sears is rated exclusively on Perfect 10 scores) went up 300 basis points the same year. Reschedules and cancels went down by 28,000 customers—that meant we gained 28,000 customers that we would not have had because we had no capacity.

The year we launched workplace visuality, our district was 47 in a field of 67. Two years later, we were number one—in the nation!

Chapter 3 Footnotes

1. For more on the topic of work culture, see Sherrie Ford's article, *On Leadership: Growing Beyond Entrepreneur* in *IndustryWeek*, June, 1999.

2. For excellent concepts and insights on like topics, see Robert Hall's *The Soul of the Enterprise: Creating a Dynamic Vision for American Manufacturing* (John Wiley & Sons, New York, N.Y., 1993).

3. For an in-depth treatment of the topic, see Robert K. Greenleaf's *Servant Leadership: A Journey into the Nature of Legitimate Power and Greatness,* (Paulist Press, Mahwah, N.J., 1977).

4. The star tetrahedron inscribed in a sphere is a familiar form in Sacred Geometry and an ancient symbol of unity found in the religious iconography of ancient Mesopotamia, Persia, India, Egypt, and China, as well as modern Judaism and Christianity (among others).

5. For an excellent detailed treatment of this theme, with many useful insights, tools, and examples, see Rick Mauer's *Caught in the Middle: A Leadership Guide for Partnership in the Workplace* (Productivity Press, Cambridge, MA, 1989).

6. Find a summary treatment of QMI's start-up requirements for launching a successful implementation in the Appendix of this book. We have found that these apply, mightily, to any improvement initiative—and are indispensable for the success of a comprehensive rollout of workplace visuality.

7. Also impressive in its effectiveness in transforming entire work cultures is the work of Dr. Sherrie Ford of Change Partners in Athens, Georgia (www.changepartners.com). See the Resource Section for more.

8. Find a brief treatment on the criticality of designated improvement time in the Appendix.

9. The 10-Doorway model, discussed in this book's third section, is fundamental to understanding— and therefore implementing—visuality in the workplace through the participation of all organizational levels. Each doorway is owned by one or several company functions (e.g., Quality, Engineering, Managers, Associates, Supervisors), with each doorway leading to a distinct visual outcome.

10. Yet, operators can only do so effectively when management provides time for improvement that is separate from production time. When QMI works on-site, we ask company managers to clarify this issue into policy before the launch, as an implementation start-up requirement (see Footnotes 6 and 8 above).

O brave new world that has such people in it.
William Shakespeare, The Tempest

The I-Driven Culture

In far too many organizations, the social fabric of the workplace—the work culture—is out of balance. Without a substantive change in that culture, no implementation, however excellent in intent, will be sustainable. And that change must begin at the level of each employee's sense of self and of his/her place within the enterprise.

Will I Be the Hero of My Own Life?

Charles Dickens opens his classic novel, *David Copperfield*, with David pondering his young life. In the quiet of his heart, he asks: "Will I be the hero of my own life?" Over the next 400 pages, David proceeds to discover the answer to that question in the trials and adventures of becoming a man in 19th century England.[1]

David's question is our question. Though quietly forgotten as we grow older, when each of us was young, this was the question in our hearts: "Will I be the hero of my own life?" It may have been worded differently. Maybe it sounded more like: "What will I be when I grow up?" Deep in the mystery of our childhood and then of our adolescent heart was a profound belief that whatever it turned out to be, "I will be excellent at it. I will excel. I will make something of my life. I will be its hero!"

This was the sentiment at the heart of a conversation I had nearly a decade ago with an employee of an aerospace manufacturer in Texas.

Ted, as I will call him, had started at the firm 27 years before, fresh out of high school. His Dad worked there before him. Ted told me that, as a kid, he would stand in the backyard and see the fighter planes cut white streamers across the sky. He remembered being thrilled, "to my bones" were his words, knowing someday he would join his Dad in making those magnificent flying machines, so slick and fast and perfect. He recalled even saying to himself, "I'm gonna makes fighter planes when I grow up! That's what I'm gonna do! Just like Dad!"

Fresh out of high school, Ted went on to say, he was hired by that great aerospace company. "I went in to be a hero, Gwendolyn," he said, "I wanted to do something great! That was 27 years ago." Ted paused; then he asked, "What happened?"

I looked at him and saw a fine person. But I knew that Ted wanted me to look deeper. He wanted me to see the hero that was still inside, waiting to get out.

I was silent.

Part of the new job description for every CEO, president, plant manager, VP, manager, and supervisor is to help employees find and manifest the hero within. Those who take this on immediately widen the definition of their own work.

Think about it. What would happen if you took this on, whether you are a floor supervisor, in charge of Finance, a production manager or the CEO of a multinational? What would happen if you committed to helping each person who reports to you become a hero in their own work? What part of your current job would stay the same? What part would change? What part of you would change?

Work Culture: Identity's Mirror

How does a manager help people realize the transformative, transcendent dimension of themselves? (Remember, we include middle managers, supervisors, executives, site managers, and union leaders in the term "manager".)

In my experience, this is, pure and simple, a matter of identity. The power to transform a traditional top-down culture into one that is empowered rests on the issue of who you believe you are—and who you believe the other person is. The deepest cultural change begins at the level of this: our beliefs about identity.

Shifting people's identify beliefs does not happen overnight and is most easily accomplished by making the process as tangible as possible, at every step. That is, management must discover ways to translate new beliefs about who people really are into a concrete system of principles, methods, and tools.

For one thing, people need time, permission, and a protocol of behavior that reliably and predictably leads them to shift into a higher dimension of their own being. You cannot help people realize the hero within merely by communicating, supporting, and encouraging. Communicate what? Support what? Encourage what? You must offer them a structure that can contain and advance the change.

That change must start on the value-add level, where so many of the distortions about people collect—misbegotten beliefs that are part and parcel of the company's current work culture. It is here that implementing visuality in the workplace can be such a potent force in transforming the entire enterprise, and with that, the work culture that every enterprise must express.

The Need to Know: The I–Driven Approach

Remember the two driving questions discussed in Chapter 2: What do I need to know? What do I need to share? The "I" in both those questions is the key to visual thinking—to finding and eliminating motion and the information deficits that trigger it through solutions that are visual.

The Need-To-Know (NTK) and Need-To-Share (NTS) are also key to creating a work culture focused on improvement. In both, the energy and power of the "I" are the driving forces. Once the "I" is systematically engaged, heroes are not far behind.

NTK and NTS happen in sequence. NTK is engaged first. "What do I need to know?" is asked and answered—visually answered—iteratively, cycle after cycle, time after time.

At the outset and for some time, the singular NTK focus is typically on the where question. Where are my pliers? Where are the parts? Where are the materials? Where are the reports? Where is my supervisor?

The result? The immediate work area is populated with dozens of visual devices that answer that individual's questions about "where." That's how the *visual where* (and the condition of automatic recoil that follows) gets deeply installed for everything that casts a shadow—through borders, home addresses, and, as applies, ID labels.

Over time, the logic of the *visual where* spreads to the entire company. The impact of this can be so far-reaching and unprecedented that people often assume that they have completed 90% of their journey to workplace visuality, even though visual order represents a mere 20% of the overall outcome. The 5S+1 method puts the first level in place, with five other visual technologies and their associated outcomes to go.

Yet, as mentioned, this physical conversion of the work environment only describes the outcome on the tangible, concrete level of the physical workflow. A second outcome surfaces which is entirely intangible—a cultural conversion that exists on the socio-leadership dimension of the enterprise.

This socio-leadership dimension impacts every layer of the workforce. For the purposes of this immediate discussion, we will look at its impact and meaning on the associate/operator/value-add level. That impact and meaning is this: *I am in control of my corner of the world.*

This is a mighty occurrence. When an operator states, "I am in control of my corner of the world" and feels in control, you can confidently predict that person is on his/her way to becoming a steady improvement contributor, a genuine citizen of the organization, and an authentic member of a high-performing team—even if that team is not yet formed. In the visual workplace, achieving visual control over one's corner of the world is the first step in mastering the rest of the physical landscape at work.

In my experience, the simple physical act of installing the *visual where* through an I–driven orientation provides us with an invaluable sense of the physical control we all crave and need in the world of work. Personal confidence is a natural by-product.

For many, this sense of control is often their first experience of any degree of mastery in the world of work. From that standpoint alone, it is a revolutionary personal breakthrough. Slowly control becomes confidence—confidence in one's own ability to address the world of work. As this sense of control and confidence spreads from individual to individual, and then from department to department, a trust in the company itself begins to emerge.

Over time (and not all that much time; several months can do the trick), these shifts in personal identity lay the groundwork for self-leadership, resourcefulness, and high levels of engagement and connection that characteristically produce high-functioning/high-performance teams.

Unless you have lived through it, it may be hard to believe that the simple act of installing the *visual where* can engender leaders where there were none before. Yet our clients, colleagues, and I have witnessed this repeatedly. The journey into visuality has to change us because it changes the way in which information is delivered—and therefore the social fabric of work.

Simply put, the liberation of information *is* the liberation of the human will. When the human will is liberated, it is free to align with any purpose that makes sense to it. Excellence attracts that will. The *liberated will* normally chooses to align with the *corporate will* if excellence is at the heart of that enterprise.

Let's delve more deeply into the presenting symptoms that make cultural transformations so tricky and so needed.

The Phases of the Identity Evolution: From Weak–I to Unified–I

As the implementation of workplace visuality deepens and spreads, we can see a parallel evolution of the "I" (the individual) in its worldly perspective from weak to strong to unified—from small to medium to great. The three phases of this evolution are summarized as:

- **Phase 1:** The Company recognizes that Weak I-s exist and are having a detrimental impact on enterprise excellence. The Company initiates a visual rollout as a remedy. The Weak I-s begin to translate their needs-to-know into visual devices (beginning with the *visual where*). In so doing, they gain a new degree of control over their workday.

- **Phase 2:** Weak I-s have now become Strong I-s, pro-actively continuing to implement high impact/low cost visual solutions in and around their work area. They continue to gather strength and exhibit strong pride in their own improvement contributions.

- **Phase 3:** Strong I-s shift their focus to the need-to-share, developing visual answers to questions that others have so that they can do their own work better. Strong I-s then become unified in their thinking and actions—informal servant leaders in their work areas. The new "I" evolves into a Team I or Unified I.

Let's walk through this process, phase by phase.

Recall our story about young Ted. Ted was like most young people when they show up for work for the first time. He felt the hero within wanting to get out; he couldn't help but bring it along everywhere he went. Years went by and connection with that hero fades. We say: People change. Indeed, most people in the workforce for more than a few years are not who they were when they began. Most are beaten and bruised by the experience we call work.

At QMI we say these folks have a Weak I. We know something of employees with Weak I-s. We know that their individual sense of self has suffered many attacks, eroding their self-esteem and ability to trust. We know that we experience them in a number of ways. Some are cynical; some non-cooperative. Others are downright nasty and belligerent; they are angry. Still others appear indifferent, unresponsive, passive, neutral or numb.

If you ask the angry ones what's wrong, they will often say that the system is "dumb"—or management doesn't know what it is doing and is ruining the company. Stupid things happen, they say, and they are powerless to stop them.

On the other end of the Weak I spectrum are people who seem indifferent. They are likely to claim that they just don't care; they will ask to be left alone. Stupid things happen, they say, and they are powerless to stop them. People from either group tend to see their work lives as out of their control and see themselves as the hapless victims of a badly-run system.

Many times, they are right. The company is badly run; dumb things do happen all the time—and everyone does seem powerless to change that. Too much goes wrong too often. Big things or little things, working seems more like walking on shifting sand than marching firmly and purposefully forward. The entire system is careening out of control, and just about everyone, including the plant manager, feels like the company is on the brink of chaos. A psychotherapist might be inspired to call the system *dysfunctional* and the people who work there *codependent*. Who would argue with that?

In strongly-aligned companies, Weak I-s are rarely a problem because they are

---

INSET 4.1: EVOLUTION OF THE "I"

Phase 1: The Company recognizes that Weak I-s exist and are having a detrimental impact on the pursuit of excellence, and determines to remedy that.

- The Weak I sees himself as a victim of the system, blaming others for an array of woes and troubles. Feeling powerless to change things, such individuals respond by either going numb or ballistic.
- Weak I-s reflect a co-dependent, passive/re-active mindset.

Phase 2: The Weak I-s: begin to translate their needs-to-know into visual devices and, in so doing, gain a degree of control over their workday.

- As this process ripens, the Weak I—the individual—has gained strength and grown independent and proud of his role in the company.
- This "I" now reflects an independent mindset and is an individual contributor (not yet team-minded).

Phase 3: The independent "I" now recognizes his need-to-share and begins to develop visual answers to questions that others have so that they can do their own work better.

- This "I" is an individual who is strong, focused, and willing to serve the greater interests of the company.
- This "I" is team-minded, with an inter-dependent mindset that recognizes that no part of the organization can succeed in isolation. That "I" embraces unity as the pathway to customer-retention and greater profit margins.

---

rarely hired. They are eliminated as candidates during the interview process—belligerent applicants for having an attitude problem, passive ones for being too shy. But in companies in the process of making (or about to make) the transition from a so-called traditional enterprise to one seeking excellence, the Weak I is typically part of the workscape, part of what is chronically wrong with the work culture, and a big (but not insurmountable) barrier to progress, prosperity, and wealth.

Moving Too Quickly to Teams

Some executives attempt to correct the organizational condition of Weak I by declaring teams into existence. This is always done with the best of intentions. The reasoning goes like this:

- Everyone has strengths.

- Everyone has weaknesses.

- If we organize people into teams, they will cover for each other's weaknesses with their strengths.

- Supervisors will be freed up to attend to larger matters.

- In the mix, we'll level the playing field and unify the workforce.

- Morale will lift; people will pay better attention to their work; they'll solve problems; we'll cut costs and improve our profit margins.

- We'll all win!

- Let's do it!

A lofty goal; but let's look at what can happen instead and often does.

The F-28 Department is asked to get into a team, appoint a team leader, and so on. Hank, Suzie, Mary, Ted, and Sam meet in a spare training room. Once the door is shut, whoever talks first, loudest and/or fastest becomes the team leader and takes over the group.

The result? Another form of the dominance hierarchy is set loose upon the company. (See the Dilbert perspective in Figure 4.1.)

You may find this scenario distorted or over-simplified. In some companies, it may be. But in others, it describes the dynamics of team-making with precision. Teams are announced, not created. And people are left to fend for themselves within the so-called team framework.

Even when companies proceed to teams with great care, supported with training and coaching, the resultant teams may not address the underlying cultural imbalance. In so many organizations, that imbalance shows up as a widespread sense of instability, no control, and disempowerment as workplace constants—the symptoms of a workforce overpopulated with Weak I-s.

How does one address this sad state? Yes, you certainly should hire for attitude and character. That is always preferred. But what do you do with folks who joined the company 10, 15, 25 years before continuous improvement became the rallying cry and enterprise excellence, the goal? They know the methods; they know the secrets; they know how to create value in the organization.

You can threaten and, if need be, fire them for not aligning with the new best thing.[2] Yet in many companies, this is not possible either because of union rules—

FIGURE 4.1: YET ANOTHER FORM OF THE DOMINANCE HIERARCHY

and/or because the expertise those ornery employees possess is indispensable. They currently hold the knowledge and know-how wealth of the enterprise—and they and you know it.

In such circumstances, company leadership often thinks it is stuck with damaged goods. Yet, there are options other than firing such people and perspectives other than feeling stuck. Seek instead a process that focuses on realigning that distorted will, strengthening that Weak I—and doing so in full cooperation with its owner, the individual him-or herself. This is the journey to a visual workplace.

The Visual Remedy: Letting the "I" Drive

Companies need a way to remedy the Weak I-s that populate the workforce, both on an associate and a management level. In companies just starting their journey to excellence, it is common for many (if not the majority) of employees to see themselves as victims of the system and powerless to change it.

Such value-add line employees are not yet ready for teams, not yet ready to pursue improvement as a group. When the work culture needs a major overhaul, look for ways that allow people to ease into an improvement frame of mind. Evolution works in this case, not revolution—even though the results, when they come, may well be revolutionary. No Kaizen Blitzes for the moment please. No requirement for the workforce to march together, single-purposed, to a greater tomorrow.

The divisiveness that is a by-product of a fragmented work culture does not convert into unity overnight. It can't be scheduled out of existence or bullied into oneness. The "I" is the starting point—the "I" in you, the "I" in me, and the "I" in the other. This is the work culture on its atomic level where it cannot be further divided. That is the level of wholeness.

The "I" exists on the level of will. That is the location in each of us of our last outpost: the will. Each of us is in charge of our own will. The outside can get close, very close to me. Other people may presume and even appropriate parts of me—my hands, my feet, my brain, even my heart—but not my will. At some point, they stop and "I" begin.

That point is the point of my will, the boundary line, a secret place of my own. This is where plans are hatched to create escape routes for the rest of me—my hands, feet, brain, and even heart. The will is the place where I am in charge. It is a place of decision, intention, and knowing. It is a place of power.

Without the will's agreement, personal progress is fraught with difficulty. With it, great things are possible. Without the alignment of the personal will with the corporate will, no company can reach the full promise of excellence. With it, the organization is unified, aligned, and ready to tackle day-to-day and long-range challenges, armed with its full potential.

The will is the powerhouse of the "I." Each person has one. And it is this that we seek to resuscitate and rehabilitate when we decide to align the work culture with excellence. When, in workplace visuality, for example, we ask individuals to install the simple formula of the *visual where* (border + home address + ID label), we empower them to make a mighty change in their immediate work environment, one that will benefit them tangibly and intangibly—and the company as well.

Not everyone agrees to do this at first. At the early stages, I–driven gives people back the right to decide if they will get on board—or not. We allow people—we ask them—to show us their stripes, as it were. We permit them to do or not do, based on their own inner calling. Many refuse. Others watch.

Yet, a few don't just get on board. Responding to their own internal vision, they cut a swath of improvement through the work landscape that can be dazzling. They create. They are unstoppable. The results are often amazing, going far beyond the simple protocol of visual order and exploding into unique visual solutions of unsurpassed usefulness and invention.

See Photo Album 6 for a set of splendid examples.

In allowing people to participate as they are inspired to—or not—we get to see who people really are, without the constant surveillance and prodding of their supervisors or managers. Remember, the whole journey is about identity. Each person must march to his own drummer and not to the participation requirements of the company—not yet.

Why, you may ask, would a company allow its employees to decide if they will get on board or not? To many a manager, this sounds far too much like *laissez-faire* or even anarchy. What business purpose can such permissiveness serve?

The answer is plain. Companies that capture and engage the hearts and minds—as well as the hands and feet—of their employees reap the harvest of a spirited, engaged and aligned workforce. The future of your profit margins depend on that.

As this chapter started out by saying: It is on the associate or value-add level that the misassumptions about identity that inhabit the work culture gravitate and collect. We begin to shift the culture there when we ask the Weak I to gain control over his or her corner of the world by implementing the *visual where* through the process known as 5S+1. Put *automatic recoil* in place: Install a border, home address, and, as applies, an ID label for everything that casts a shadow.

This protocol is simple. It is knowable; and it is largely do-able within the workday. Bit by bit, tool by tool, part by part, shelf by shelf, the Weak I gains some control, some power, over his/her corner of the world and grows in personal stature as well.

Yet, take note: When, in this process, we invite employees to follow their own lead, their own preferences, we do so exclusively about participating in improvement activity. Such an invitation is not made in reference to production performance. We cannot and do not tolerate any slackening of workload, quality or delivery requirements. Those demands are as uncompromising as ever. They do not waiver.

What becomes elective for the employee at the start of the rollout is the decision to participate in improvement or not. Why? Because it is important that we discover what people will do when the pressure is off—when, for all intents and purposes, they are encouraged to participate in improvement or not, based on their own personal preferences, on their own inner calling. We must allow them to find and re-claim their own will.

This is not as radical as it sounds—people already exercise that right. You may get them to show up, but they won't bring much else with them. They won't bring their full resources to bear. They show up; they comply. But they will not initiate; and they will not own. They will be passive. Or they will pretend to be involved; but the results will be pale by comparison with what is possible.

Yet, companies are often grateful for pale results, in the face of its alternative:

Photo Album 6

Visual Inventiveness at United Electric

Creating Visual Thinkers at United Electric Controls (UEC)

United Electric Controls (Watertown, MA) is an ISO-certified company that battles daily in the highly competitive switch and controls market where precision, quality, and low-cost are givens. Today, UEC is a cellular manufacturing jewel, with a motivated, articulate, and inventive workforce and supervisors who are first and foremost superb coaches. Launching workplace visuality in 1993 was one of UEC's first improvement commitments.

BILL ANTUNES

A BUYER USING BILL'S DISPLAY

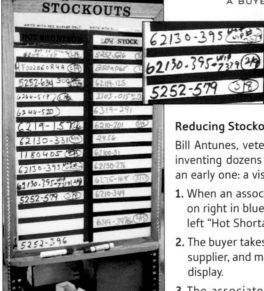

Reducing Stockouts through Visual Displays

Bill Antunes, veteran UEC assembler, is responsible for inventing dozens of remarkable visual solutions. Here's an early one: a visual display for part shortages.

1. When an associate notices a part is low, she marks it on right in blue "Low Stock"—or if out, then in red on left "Hot Shortage."

2. The buyer takes note on his daily rounds, contacts the supplier, and marks the promised delivery date on the display.

3. The associate then circles the date, both to say thanks and to complete the communication loop.

Bill's display replaced a 3-part memo system the company had used for years. It also led to buyers actually visiting the areas they supported—instead of associates sending memos to them. A few years later, all UEC buyers moved their desks onto the production floor.

Paperwork Improvement through Visual Order

From the moment in 1993 when John Pacheco, veteran machinist at UEC, was first trained in workplace visuality, he never stopped inventing visual solutions. This brilliant paperwork mini-system captures many visual principles.

Before ⬆

John realized that he did not need an eight-foot table for his paperwork; he got rid of it.

After—1 ▸

Removing a shelf from a nearby rack, John replaced it with a wooden shelf on sliders—getting double duty out of a pre-existing value field and allowing him to pull the paperwork function to him when needed and store it out of the way the rest of the time.

After—2 ▸

Fresh paint plus borders and home addresses complete the system, still in use ten years later.

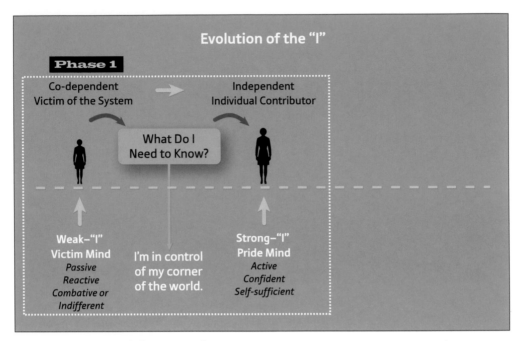

FIGURE 4.2: PHASE I—THE SHIFT FROM WEAK-I TO STRONG-I

nothing. But so much more is possible when the will is more fully engaged. When people *have* to, they do—they obey. When people *want* to, they create—they feel pride, even joy.

When people can find *themselves* in the change, they own it deeply. They I–dentify with it and it is theirs.

Figure 4.2 shows the progression from the Weak I to the Strong I. The shift happens when the person applies the need-to-know and gains control over his/her corner of the world.

Another way of saying this is that the person finds a sense of safety, sanity and stability at work.

Once that control is established, something very beautiful and natural happens. The person turns to others and says, "How may I help you? What do I need to share? What do I know that you need to know—in order for you to do your work?" This is the shift that occurs in Phase 2 (Figure 4.3). In this second stage of the change, the person builds on the security gained in getting control of his corner of the world and finds he can afford to think of others. And she does.

The resulting visual solutions answer the questions that others have in the work

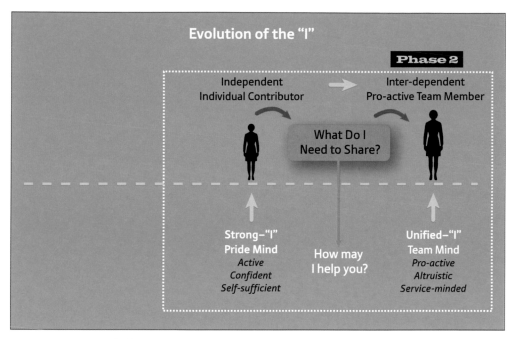

FIGURE 4.3: PHASE 2—THE SHIFT FROM STRONG-I TO UNIFIED-I

area. These others may be internal and external suppliers, internal and external customers, co-workers, and/or management.

At this stage of workplace visuality, the individual has already aligned his personal will with the interests of the corporation and serves in the role of informal leader. This is when the corporation reaps huge cultural and bottom-line benefits from its patience and forbearance during Phase 1, when the "I" elected to get on board—or not to.

Look at Figure 4.4 to see the entire progression—both phases. These are simple, subtle, and powerful changes that are able to impact one of the most elusive aspects of enterprise excellence: the individual will, the "I".

Rowers, Watchers, Grumblers: Another Perspective on the "I"

It doesn't take too many improvement initiatives to discover that people tend to respond to change in one of three ways: They embrace it; they resist it; or they don't have an opinion about it one way or the other—they are neutral. At QMI we call this threesome: The Rowers, Watchers, and Grumblers.[3] They offer us another per-

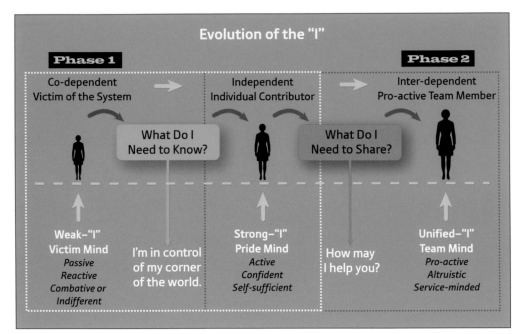

FIGURE 3.4: THE EVOLUTION OF THE "I" (BOTH PHASES)

spective on the "I".

Rowers are the early contributors. Self-starters and independent by nature, they move ahead, heedless of barriers. They see the vision, the possibilities, burning brightly before them and just keep rowing. While they may not yet act as a unifying force in the company, they are pro-active and confident.

Watchers hang back and let others (the Rowers) blaze the trail. Then, if nothing bad happens to the frontrunners, they may join in, however tentatively, or just continue to watch. Watchers make no deliberate effort to obstruct change (the way, as we will see, Grumblers do). Yet they also do not easily lend it their enthusiasm. For Watchers to engage, they have to be convinced that they are safe and that the change is strongly and tangibly supported by management. They don't like taking chances. They are not resisters but suffer, instead, from the cultural impediment called inertia. Given reliable conditions, Watchers often become Rowers.

Grumblers, on the other hand, are past masters at being grumpy in ways that everyone will notice. They whine, complain, moan, groan, refuse, sulk, reject, deny, and sometimes outright sabotage just about any improvement effort. And in all of this, they also like to grandstand, making sure, one suspects, that we notice their displeasure. They watch keenly for our response to their resistance. They seem fully aware that many an upstanding person will want to help them change their ways and, as it were, "save them from themselves."

Grumblers are very good at grabbing our attention—and they expect us to give it. When we do, we make a fatal mistake. Instead of accepting our concern as an invitation to parley, Grumblers use it to take us for a ride, their ride. And when they have had their way with us—meaning, we get even more wrapped up in the hope of reforming them—they walk away and send the unmistakable message that they are indeed incorrigible and happy to stay that way. Grumblers are completely in charge of their own will; and if they can, they will also take over ours.

When push comes to shove, the only progressive course of action, long-term, is to concentrate on keeping the Rowers rowing. Watchers will continue to watch. When and if they see the boat is steady and has sprung no leaks, they will likely put a crooked smile on their face and pick up an oar or two.

The Grumbler will continue to act very grumpy and resistive. Yet, it is just as likely that, after a while, he or she will do an about-face and become a formidable pace-setting Rower. If you ask why the sudden change of heart, the erstwhile Grumbler is likely to declare, "I changed my mind," and then walk away.

In this regard, Grumblers are exactly right. Since they are in charge of their own will, they get to decide how they want to use it. As Grumblers, they are exasperating—as Rowers, inspiring.

There are many lessons here but the primary one is and always will be to keep the Rowers rowing, knowing that Watchers and Grumblers will come along, when and as they are ready.

It should go without saying that at some point in a company's journey to excellence, people who are actively obstructive have to be dismissed.

People are Worth the Pause

Experience has taught us, however, that people are worth the pause—a small period of time when they are truly allowed, even encouraged, to be themselves, with no fear of penalty. They are shown a new way and then allowed that little bit of extra time to find the path—or not. In this we discover yet another dimension of the I–driven approach.

People can only authentically be themselves. Active/passive, cooperative/resis-

Photo Album 7

Kanban and Visual Inventiveness

I-Driven Visual Inventiveness at Plymouth Tube

With eight metalworking mills and some 900 employees, Plymouth Tube Company (Warrenville, IL) is a manufacturer of high-precision tubes and extruded shapes. Committed to implementing workplace visuality, lean, and other improvement strategies, Plymouth started its journey to manufacturing excellence in 1999. It continues it to this day.

ROBIN GRIGGS

Stock outages and parts hoarding had become a problem at Plymouth Tube in West Monroe, LA when Robin Griggs, supplies purchaser, developed the kanban replenishment system you see in this album.

Robin came up with several innovations to make the system work locally. First, because parts bins in this rack were so small, Robin installed a timecard holder on each side of the rack for kanban cards. Follow the numbered captions for more.

1. Welding parts are stored in cubbies in this rack.

2. Each bin is marked with the part number plus min/max levels.

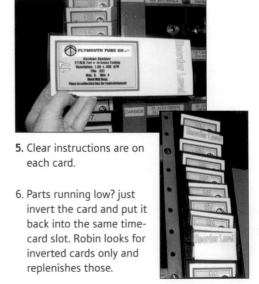

3. Cards are numbered to correspond to each small bin.

4. The card slot is numbered too.

5. Clear instructions are on each card.

6. Parts running low? just invert the card and put it back into the same time-card slot. Robin looks for inverted cards only and replenishes those.

tive, enthusiastic/grumpy, aggressive/indifferent—if the individual is simply met where he or she is and accepted as such, the chances of change increase, whether those changes are triggered by self-reflection or outside feedback.

The workplace is not a therapist couch. It is also not populated with perfect beings. Cultures in transition have many lessons to learn and huge treasures to unearth. Those treasures are hidden in the congestion and complexity of the flow of material and information in and through the facility. Treasures can also be found in the temporarily complex and congested hearts and minds of the people who have given 10, 20, 30 years of their lives to your company.

When material congestion looked like a way of life under that roof, these people stuck it out. They took the hits. They persevered. They got bruised in the process. So it is fitting and right for us to provide them with the time, structure, and support they need to make the same transition within themselves that the physical workplace is undergoing on its journey to excellence. Your employees want that excellence too.

One of the great business thinkers of our times, Bruce Hamilton, put it this way in the Foreword of my book, *Smart Simple Design*: "We were changing the way things were done, and we were changing ourselves in the process." Such victories are hard won, and they are mighty in their harvest.

We end this chapter as we began. People want to be heroes. We want the hero that we came to know in our heart when we were very young to go to work with us. We want the hero to show up there. Yet, if the company has made no room for heroes, has no structured way through which that hero can be uncovered and revealed, it shrinks in us—even as we shrink at work.

I have found no better framework than the technologies of the visual workplace to bring this extraordinary outcome into fruition, equally across the entire organization. The change begins on the associate level because, as stated repeatedly, the value-add level acts as a magnet and a mirror for all the misconceptions and imbalances in the work culture. That is one of its functions.

If change is to happen at all, it must start from the ground up. In starting there, we have the chance to reconstitute the foundation of the enterprise and the fundamental definition of identity—yours, his, hers, ours, theirs, and mine.

Chapter 4 Footnotes

1. My thanks to Swami Chetanananda for making this connection for me. See his book, *Will I Be the Hero of My Own Life?* (Rudra Press, 1995). Available from the Rudra Press website: www.rudrapress.com.

2. In yet other companies, a deep sense of stewardship and servant leadership on the executive level mitigates against such a response.

3. My thanks to Dr. Ryuji Fukuda for the original version of this useful story. For much more on Rowers, Watchers and Grumblers, see Chapter 7 in my book, *Visual Systems: Harnessing the Power of a Visual Workplace* (Amacom, 1997). Available from the QMI website: www.visualworkplace.com.

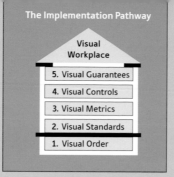

FIGURE 1

Section | Three

TECHNOLOGIES OF THE VISUAL WORKPLACE

In this third section of the book, we delve into two constructs that help us understand visuality as a destination and show us ways to get there.

The first is the framework known as the technologies of the visual workplace: a discrete set of methods, tools, and visual outcomes that comprehensively convert the physical environment into a visual one. Though many of these methods will be familiar to you, what may be new is thinking about them as a single line logic and an integrated framework that shares a common purpose: to share vital information about the task at hand at-a-glance, without speaking a word—in short, to let the workplace speak.

These technologies represent a progression, a continuum of information of sharing, that group into five major categories, read from the bottom up as you would a ladder, with each rung having its own distinct operational purpose until the progression culminates in a fully-functioning visual workplace (Figure 1 above). This is the

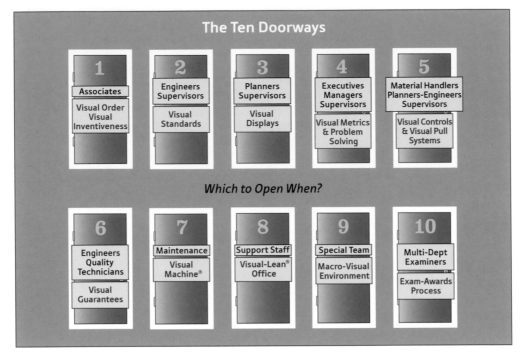

The Ten Doorways

1	2	3	4	5
Associates	**Engineers Supervisors**	**Planners Supervisors**	**Executives Managers Supervisors**	**Material Handlers Planners-Engineers Supervisors**
Visual Order Visual Inventiveness	Visual Standards	Visual Displays	Visual Metrics & Problem Solving	Visual Controls & Visual Pull Systems

Which to Open When?

6	7	8	9	10
Engineers Quality Technicians	**Maintenance**	**Support Staff**	**Special Team**	**Multi-Dept Examiners**
Visual Guarantees	Visual Machine®	Visual-Lean® Office	Macro-Visual Environment	Exam-Awards Process

FIGURE 2: THE TEN DOORWAYS INTO A VISUAL WORKPLACE

Implementation Pathway.

At QMI, we use this pathway in two important ways—first, to diagnose the current level of visual competency in an organization and then, second, as a roadmap for planning how to improve it.

The second framework that helps us achieve enterprise-wide visuality is the *Ten Doorways into Workplace Visuality* (Figure 2). Each doorway is linked to a different group of employees. Each group owns and opens a different doorway and develops a different category of visual function—a given technology of the visual workplace. The group in charge of a door leads the way into that particular form of visual information sharing and is held accountable for that outcome.

Using the Ten Doorways as a guide, the organization can make sure that everyone—all members of the workforce—get directly involved in asking and visually answering the need-to-know/need-to-share questions, from the viewpoint of the individual "I."

In the next three chapters, these two frameworks are jointly presented as we discuss the various levels of visuality—in sequence—and the group responsible for implementing each.

"Visual Order is like 5S on steroids!"
Aleta Sherman
Boulder, Colorado

CHAPTER 5

Visual Order: Visuality's Foundation

The first level of the Implementation Pathway to the visual workplace is visual order, the doorway that is wholly owned by line-associates—those employees who work on the value-add level.

Apply the process called 5S+1 and produce the outcome called visual order (Figure 5.1), also known as the *visual where* and automatic recoil.

Do not confuse visual order with industrial housekeeping (workplace organization)—or the 5S+1 method that produces visual order with 5Ss, 6Ss or 4Ds. They are very different.

The differences are both in content (knowledge) and the implementation approach to apply that content (know-how). I do not mean to suggest that the QMI system is superior to all others. It does, however, have several core elements that make it distinctive from the others. Based on the results of dozens of successful implementations, they produce highly effective and sustainable outcomes

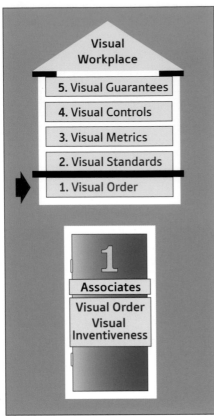

across a range of work settings.

For one, there is a sizeable difference in what the Ss actually ask us to do. The five words that comprise 5S in Japan can be translated any number of ways. Early in the 1980s, shortly after I joined Productivity Inc. (then the premier western source for books and other material on the Japanese manufacturing miracle), I was asked to find five English words that could serve as equivalents to the five Japanese words. What I came up with will probably be familiar to you as they have appeared in many Productivity Inc. books:

- *Seiri:*   Sort
- *Seison:*   Shine
- *Seiso:*   Set in Order
- *Seiketsu:*   Standardize
- *Shitsuke:*   Sustain

In the early 1990s, when I left Productivity Inc. to start my own company, Quality Methods International, I re-translated the Japanese Ss into actionable steps that produced reliable outcomes (Figure 5.2). I do not tell you this to share a nugget of my personal history. I tell you to alert you to the fact that 5S must make sense in the language of your workforce. Otherwise, 5S can remain largely unimplementable, however much time and effort you and your colleagues invest in trying.

The Goal is Visuality

The Japanese use 5S to establish and maintain a clear, clean, and orderly workplace. That works well in Japan and in Japanese transplants throughout the world. This approach to 5S, however, often does not work that well in western companies. Even when an initial advantage is gained, it can end there, be unsustainable or require excessive effort to keep it in place. Why? you may ask.

For one thing, in nearly 25 years of implementation, I have never been very successful in rallying people around the notion of *neat/clean/orderly*, at least not enough to base an implementation on it. As for getting adults to clean up after themselves, I am not their Mother and they know it.

When I would try to talk about the importance of cleanliness and order as an outcome, I could not help but notice that some people (usually the women) got very animated in favor—while others just tuned me out (often the men). The group was

5S+1: Visual Order	
S1	Sort Through/Sort Out
S2	Scrub the Workplace
S3	Secure Safety
S4	Select Locations
S5	Set Locations
+1	Sustain 5S+1 Habit

FIGURE 5.2: 5S+1-VISUAL ORDER

polarized even before we got started. As a result, I decided that *neat/clean/orderly* was a battle I no longer wanted to fight; I knew I would lose.

Instead, I began to speak to people about *implementing visuality*—installing visual answers to the six core questions, beginning with the *visual where*. The clean up part, I explained, was done in order to prepare the physical work environment to hold visual information. Never again did I attempt to make clean or cleanliness independent outcomes.

That is the reason I sought a different name for what 5S produced as an outcome. I could see that it was more that mere industrial housekeeping or workplace organization. Done correctly, the process establishes the foundation for the entire visual progression and, as discussed in the last two chapters, puts the cultural groundwork in place for a truly empowered enterprise. We coined the term: *5S+1: Visual Order.*®

A decade later, the 5S+1 process continues to focus on workplace visuality as the outcome, not cleanliness, neatness or order. In visual order, as with all pathway outcomes, the emphasis is on creating greater visuality in the workplace, not on promoting the method that produces that. Naming the outcome you want—not the process used—is crucial for gaining buy-in and getting people on board and rowing.

I see a parallel in this when I look at that perfect little black size 10 dress in my closet that I wore once to a fancy dinner. There it sits, surrounded by the 12s and 14s I currently use to cover my body. I know that I will need to eat a heck of a lot of cottage cheese and fruit to get that little black dress to fit me again. Yet, if I keep thinking about cottage cheese and fruit, and not about that little black dress—and how fantastic I looked in it, not so very long ago—I will never get there. I will get bored and bail. So I keep my thought on that little black dress. That keeps me going.

To me, asking people to do another round of 5S is like asking them to have some more cottage cheese and fruit. What's the joy in that? Why should they bother?

Companies complain that their 5S initiative is dying on the vine. "We can't seem to keep people interested," they tell me. Could it be because what they are asking people to do is not all that interesting? Could it be that they are trying to motivate people by naming the method instead of the outcome? That's a big part of why companies get stuck. In addition, when management fails to link the 5Ss with visuality, 5S will almost certainly get implemented in isolation of the more advanced forms of visual information sharing.

Visual order jumps over these pitfalls and urges us to implement the *visual where* thoroughly—for everything that casts a shadow. Install workplace visuality. Invent visual solutions. Implement visual functionality. 5S+1 raises the amps and fires the imagination: "Hey everyone, we are going to create a dazzling demonstration of what visuality looks like in this area and how it gets implemented." Now that's a rallying cry. That's something people can run with, a vision that calls to them on a much deeper level.

As Aleta Sherman, a colleague in Colorado, once remarked, *"Visual order is like 5S on steroids!"* She got it right!

Visual Order

The purpose of 5S+1 is to prepare the physical environment to hold visual information and then to install visual location information—the *visual where*—for everything that casts a shadow: border, home address, and, as applies, ID label. This is what it means to install visual order. This simple formula creates an exceptional outcome called *automatic recoil:* the ability of every workplace item to find its way back to its designated home, based solely on the visual location information built on it and into it—border, home address and, as applies, ID label.

As we now walk through the method, step by step, you'll see further points of comparison between 5S+1 and other related methods—differences in emphasis, content, and outcome.

S1: Sort Through/Sort Out

The first step in the process tells us to get rid of the "junk"—anything people say they don't want or need to support their work (Figure 5.3). These get removed from the value field and put into the local red-tag corner.

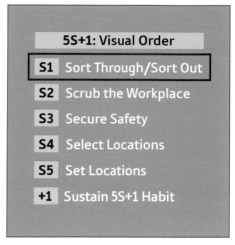

FIGURE 5.3:
SORT THROUGH/SORT OUT

Sorting through stuff and sorting it out is an indispensable first step in preparing the workplace for visual information; and it can be a lot of fun. When done routinely, say once a quarter (or a month) after the initial sorting, it is also a good maintenance tool. This tool works equally well for office environments, except that support staff generally prefer to name what they want to keep rather than what to get rid of.

S1/Sort is a simple and powerful first step in preparing the work environment for visual information—with one mighty hurdle to jump. The hurdle is directly linked to the I-driven nature of the change. The decision of what stays and what goes in one's own personal workspace is strictly up to the "I". If the item is in a common space or shared, then tagging is used, not as a voting device but in order to surface people's preferences.

Going back to the discussion in Chapter 4 on the power of the "I" and the mistake that many companies make in moving to teams prematurely, we do not use S1 to jam a team into place. The same is true if we are tempted to use red-tagging as a way to vote. Don't! When red-tagging is used as voting, we turn our collective backs on the primacy of the "I" and diminish its ability to help empower the workforce and bring the organization into balance.

This is a subtle point of tremendous implication. Voting automatically polarizes those who vote. That is implicit in its use. Individuals who do not yet have strong self-concepts, who have not yet made their way back from the vagaries and abuses of the obedience model (the command and control/top-down approach) will crumple under such a vote—or go ballistic.

Why chance it? What do you gain in forcing the issue to a vote? More importantly, what do you lose? If red-tagging is used as a proxy for voting, then the majority will rule and, whatever the fate of the item, everyone will know that noth-ing in the enterprise related to empowerment has fundamentally changed.

We make this point absolutely clear when we assist a company in an on-site implementation. To executives and associates alike, our position on this matter is unwavering. We say it this way:

"I lied to you before when I said the first 'S' is for Sort Through/Sort Out. I lied. It isn't. The first 'S' is for Spirit."

(If you gag at the notion of spirit in the workplace, you might prefer stating that the "first S is for Respect" because that, in great part, is the meaning behind the phrase—respect for the individual. Then again, respect doesn't begin with an "S." What to do?)

When we say the first "S" is for Spirit, we refer to the spirit of the workplace and the spirit inside each of us, equally. When a company uses red-tagging as a vote, it turns S1 and the journey to workplace visuality into a battleground. The tribal majority will certainly win that battle; the offending item will be removed from the area. But the war will be lost—the war against waste, the war against motion that all those hundreds and thousands of "I"s are intended to wage. The victory of a fully empowered and unified enterprise will elude us again. And to that we say, "Sigh."

This is a great loss. It is tied to not understanding the mechanics of implement-ing visual order or the power of the very first S (Sort Through/Sort Out) to wreck havoc on the entire future of the initiative, if incorrectly implemented. At this early stage, every step must be carefully placed, most especially the first step. Once again, the Chinese proverb hits the nail exactly on the head: "The first step of the journey *is* the destination."

Never forget that red-tagging brings everyone face-to-face with one of the most challenging aspects of changing the physical workplace: a personal sense of owning the things in the workplace and sometimes the location itself, even though—tech-nically speaking—they are all company assets. People live at work. For eight to ten hours a day, this is home to your employees—and to you too. When you undertake to physically change the physical workplace, you smack up against one of the strongest human instincts. It's called the territorial imperative; and it sounds like this: "Take your mitts off that thing! It's mine!"

Here at this first step of a very long journey to workplace visuality and an aligned and spirited enterprise, the company has everything to gain and nothing to lose in letting the values of the I-driven approach govern the seemingly mundane decision: Do we throw that thing out or let it stay?

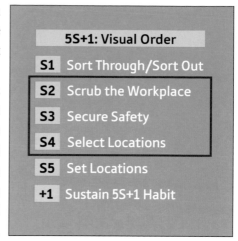

The moment crackles with possibility. People watch. People wait. What will you do? What will the enterprise embrace? The old way (do as I say) or the new (the first S is for Spirit)? A great deal is at stake. Decide in favor of the "I," and you break the inertia of the past. The hidden pyramid is pried free of its authoritarian counterpart and can begin the inversion process. Decide against the "I" and the habit of using power as a weapon strengthens.

A great deal is at stake.

An effective implementation of visual order serves multiple purposes, across many dimensions of work life. For the production floor and the physical reality of the workplace, it brings order that you can see, order that functions. On a macro-cultural level, visual order is capable of converting a traditional work culture to one that can promote and support enterprise excellence. It installs an improvement infrastructure and puts an end to myths that say there is no time to improve.

On a micro-cultural level, visual order provides an opening for individual employees, starting on the operator/line level, to reconstruct, rehabilitate, and restore a brilliant sense of self and one's own personal power to do, change, and contribute.

These are mighty outcomes and they are real. Their impact is powerfully felt on the bottom line. Why throw them away for the sake of a red-tag item? Just remember: *The First S is for Spirit.* For an S1 story of inspired leadership and another of misbegotten understanding, see Inset 5.1.

S2: Shine The Workplace and Everything in It

When people start to clean in S2, they do so in order to prepare the surfaces to hold visual information. First borders, home addresses, and ID labels—and later more

INSET 5.1: EXECUTIVES AND MANAGERS—KEEPERS OF THE FLAME

There is a moment in every implementation when the future of the initiative hangs in the balance. It is an exact moment, a moment when the values of the new way run smack up against those of the old. When that moment comes, sponsors of rollout must act swiftly and decisively in favor of the change they are seeking. Here are two vignettes—one inspires, the other shocks.

S1 and the Potted Palm

PHOTO 5. 1:
DOROTHY AND THE PALM

The first Visual Workplace training session at Parker Denison in Marysville, Ohio was not easy. The thirty union associates in the room had heard it all before and were not buying any of it.

After the session closed, I walked around the floor and made contact again with the participants. Dorothy Walls and Sheila Bowersmith, two accomplished machine operators, showed me a scrawny potted palm sitting in a plastic pot; they were nursing it slowly back into life. (I made a mental note to bring in a beautiful Italian ceramic I was no longer using to offer as a better home for it and its three scrawny shoots.)

A month later, on-site for session two, I stopped by before the group convened to see Dorothy, Sheila, and the palm. "Where's the palm?" I asked, "I have this new pot for it." I held out the Italian ceramic.

"Oh they killed it," Dorothy said. "What?" I squeaked. "What on earth do you mean?" "Oh, we put a sign on it," said Shelia, "when we were doing S1: 'Keep your paws off our potted palm!'" We thought it was funny but someone must have taken offense. The next day it was dead—someone sprayed it with weed killer." They sighed, smiling weakly.

I looked at both of them and said, "Excuse me. I'll be back." I went straight to the office of Ken Theiss, the GM. "May I come in? Something has happened," I said. "What's up?" said Theiss. "There's been a murder in your plant," I said. "What!" said Ken. "Yes," said I, "Someone killed Dorothy's and Shelia's potted palm." I held my breath, knowing that whatever Ken said next would either advance the visual conversion or set it back, way back. The values of the change were at stake. What would he say?

Ken said exactly the right thing! He said this: "I knew that plant . . . (long pause). Tell me what happened." I told him. Without a another word, Ken stood up, walked straight to Dorothy and Sheila and declared that this kind of behavior would not be tolerated in his company. Within moments the word spread.

Things were different after that. Oh they still went slow, and there were plenty of bumps. But a new level of respect was at its foundation. Respect for the change that wanted to happen. And Mr. Theiss bought Dorothy and Sheila a new potted palm. They put it in the fancy Italian ceramic. It is alive to this day.

S1 and Daddy's Little Girls

In a different union plant, one that will remain unnamed, management launched an industrial housekeeping process (not 5S+1). The consultants that led the change put special emphasis on discipline, audits, and adhering to standards. An early standard forbade personal items at work. Not surprisingly the workforce pushed back. Management decided to take a stand. During the graveyard shift, day-shift production managers walked the floor and threw out every personal item they found.

Some years later, QMI began an implementation there and met with terrific resistance. Within months, one of the machinists filed a grievance against me, which the union committee quickly dropped. I remained puzzled as to my offense.

About three years later, when the implementation had taken hold and nearly everyone was rowing and involved in the visual conversion, the machinist who had filed the grievance (whom I happened to think was a terrific guy) took me aside, to apologize. I told him that was not necessary; I knew I could be a bit of a handful and not too worry. "No, that's not it," he said. "Let me explain." I listened.

He told me about the previous attempt to "5S" the plant. Then he added detail. He said, "I have three girls. For years when they were very small, my girls used to put little love notes in my lunch box. I'd find them every day and tape them on my tool box. One night about six years ago, a production manager I'd known for years went into my tool box and threw all those notes away. All of them. Without my permission. In the name of 5S. Because his manager told him to. I came in the next day and they were gone. I was very angry. But I needed my job. I have three kids."

"When you showed up talking about 5S, I thought it was the same thing all over again, and I took it out on you. It's not the same thing. I'm sorry."

I was speechless, moved by his apology for which there was no need and appalled by the story. The values-disconnect that the company had demonstrated in the name of progress, in the name of 5S, was extreme. I had seen the kind of missionary zeal many 5S approaches push. "Just Do It!" was a familiar battle cry—easy to spout but risky to implement and sustain. I am sure the company thought these were the secret driving principles of the change they wanted. Yet how could they be, when those principles asked managers to do to others what would have outraged them if it had been done to them.

S1 is the first step of the first step of a very long journey. If there is a place where a visual initiative can go off the tracks with little hope of recovery, it is exactly here. Remember managers and executives: The First "S" is for Spirit—and you are the keeper of that flame.

> *Discipline is remembering what you love.* —Albert Einstein

advanced visual devices and systems.

They are not asked to clean to make me, their boss or God happy. They are not asked to clean to demonstrate that they are capable of discipline, at least not discipline in the usual sense of that word, with all its heavy cultural overlays. People are asked to clean in order to prepare the physical workplace so that it can hold visual information. That's it—and that's all. Information won't stick on dust, grease or grime.

Managers regularly get obsessed with cleanliness and order, but rarely line personnel or anyone who actually has to do the cleaning, day after day. This is not to say that cleaning cannot be made fun; I have participated in many fun-filled cleaning blitzes. And this is not to deny that some employees find genuine satisfaction in cleaning and in keeping things clean—but not all.

In S2, we ask people to clean it once and clean it good, and look for ways to never ever have to clean the darn thing again. People look for ways to prevent dirt. Here the I-driven dynamic is seen as the "I" in I-nvent. The results are excellent.

S3: Secure Safety

S3 is all about increasing the safety quotient at work. As the saying goes, *Safety is cheap. Accidents are expensive.* Area operators are asked to notice risk and to correct what they can themselves. Anything else gets reported to the company's Safety Team or Committee—and shame on any company that does not have one.

Here again, with the premium put on visual inventiveness, people in the area come up with amazing innovative safety solutions to risks that sometimes only they recognize.

See Photo Album 8 for visual solutions linked to S2 and S3 from the Trailmobile/Canada implementation.

S4: Select Locations

S4/Select Locations is about *smart placement*—deciding where workplace items should be located, based on accelerating the flow of material, information, and people in and through the work area. S4 is the area's chance to verify or improve

LEFT
FIGURE 5.5:
WHAT-IS MAP
(ARTIST RENDERING)

RIGHT
FIGURE 5.6:
DREAM MAP

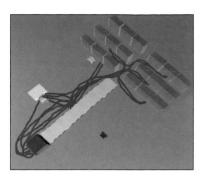

the position of things before those spots are locked in place in the next step of the process—S5/Set Locations—through borders, home addresses, and, if applicable, ID labels.

The principle that governs this placement is: *Function plus location equals flow*.

S4/Select Locations is another one of those departure points in the QMI process that distinguishes it from other 5S methods. In it, area associates take on the work that is usually reserved for engineers, cellular design, and/or a Kaizen Blitz. This is a powerful opportunity for value-add employees to re-think, re-imagine, and re-layout their own work and their own work area.

In undertaking this, line employees construct two maps. The first, called the What-Is Map, is a map of the area as it is now, with all items placed as they are now. After that placement is secured, the team traces out the many streams of motion that current layout triggers: Function plus location equals flow. (See Figure 5.5 for a much-cleaned up artist's representation of a What-Is Map.)

The second, called the Could-Be or Dream Map, shows the exact same area but with easy-to-move items and WIP relocated to better support an accelerated flow. Again, motion is traced, only this time it is visibly reduced because the new layout reflects placement to support an accelerated flow (Figure 5.6, again, an artist's representation).

The Dream Map is an opportunity for value-add employees to rearrange their work area for their own convenience—that is, so that flow quickens, travel distance is shortened, and motion is greatly reduced or even eliminated.

Area associates present both maps, with their insights and recommendations, to senior management for comment, appreciation, and, as needed, authorization.

Time and again, the S4 Mapping process produces tangible breakthroughs in layout comparable to those triggered in a Kaizen Blitz. The result is the same

Photo Album 8

S2 + S3 Solutions at Trailmobile/Canada

Using Visuality to Turn a Plant Around

Under the leadership of Tom Wiseman, Trailmobile launched a visual rollout in 1999 in its newly-acquired facility in Toronto. At that time, the monthly accident rate was at an astonishing 46.2%; operational efficiency, 86%; and pre-delivery warranty costs, $40,000.

Within eight months of the launch, monthly employee absenteeism was down from 80% to 10%—and a previously disconnected and troubled workforce began to move as one.

Roof Mezzanine

The trailer roof gets installed from the mezzanine. Several times a shift, large barrels of trash and scrap are carried down the steep stairs for disposal—risky even for the two men this required. ▶

◀ Roof Team
Salam Azar, Tyler France, Paul Russel, and Ed Alvez.

◀ ▲ S2 Motion-Busters

Look at the simple but brilliant pair of S2 solutions the Roof Team installed, once visual order and motion were understood: two chutes cut into the mezzanine floor, one for scrap, one for trash. Broad yellow borders, plus a lid on the trash chute and metal barrier around the scrap chute (painted red for safety), complete this excellent S2 (motion-prevention) system.

Expect Trackable and Impressive Bottom Line Benefits

The visual implementation continued, area by area. 100 visual thinkers later: 50% of the total production floor was liberated and re-deployed; operational efficiency was at 117%; pre-delivery warranty costs were down over 95%; and accident frequency was down by nearly 75%. Then, when gas prices rose, the market dried up, and the plant had to cut back to one shift (50% fewer employees), the workforce sustained the 117% efficiency and increased it by 7%.

I don't believe I have ever participated in a visual conversion of such speed, precision, alignment or joy. I remember it with tremendous gratitude.

This visual workplace rollout has unlocked the potential of our employees. The potential was always there. We just couldn't see it.

Now associates are the driving force behind not just change but our journey to excellence. And new employees can light a candle from an existing flame where before there was nothing.

> April Love
> Director of Continuous Improvement (former)
> Trailmobile/Canada

Visual Safety Solution

Several times a day, sheets of steel are delivered to the stamping machine (above). But, in backing up to the machine, drivers would often bump against the yellow stays (left) that support the fabrication of the trailer floor, endangering the riveters. When the stays were painted a more visible color—red, the problem disappeared.

The S2 and S3 solutions shown here represent the tiniest window on the remarkable visual inventiveness of the Trailmobile/Canada workforce.

tremendous cost savings and safety improvements.

Yet the non-tangible benefits are equally impressive. S4 Mapping is the first time that associates—who heretofore have not been required to align with other area associates—now find themselves sharing ideas and collaborating on building an accurate current area map and imagining a future one. The spirit of team begins to emerge.[1]

By the time the Maps are completed, ownership of the physical change is high. After the presentation to management, the group goes about the work of matching the actual layout with the Dream Map. That in place, they are now ready to lay down the borders and home addresses that capture that new layout in visual function. They are ready for *S5/Set Locations.*

S5: Set Locations

Culturally speaking, by the time the department reaches S5/Set Locations, everyone—including value-add associates—has a pretty good feel for who rows, watches or grumbles. This information is not a problem. It is simply information.

When it comes time to lay the borders down, those who are enthusiastic will remain so. Those who watch will laugh or smirk. Those who grumble will either say rude things or go bananas. Borders are not readily understood by people who have not ever worked in a company where visual order has been installed comprehensively.

Borders, in fact, are the single most important physical element of your pursuit of the *visual where*—your pursuit of order, orderliness, retrievability, and automatic recoil.

The formula for automatic recoil is as simple as it is powerful: a border, home address and, if applicable, an ID label. Start on the floor and move up and in as you install the *visual where* on walls, on benches and other work surfaces, on shelving, and in cabinets and drawers. In short, automatic recoil gets installed for everything that casts a shadow.[2]

This mandate applies equally to items that are easily moveable and those that are not, such as machines and tall shelves. Yes, when we say everything that casts a shadow, we do mean it.

Photo Album 9 shows you examples of automatic recoil on the floor level, on work surfaces, and in drawers and cabinets—and illustrates several key S5 principles and practices.

Bordering usually gets off to a slow start. First, some people don't really think you mean it or want it. Other people think it's just plain nutty. The idea seems odd primarily because few people have ever worked in a company that adopted borders as part of its improvement strategy.

It does not take long, however, for everyone to experience the power of borders for themselves.

Long before borders get laid, technical decisions need to be in place: The color-coding system (minimum of five, maximum of nine); plastic tape versus paint versus Durastripe[3]; how to put borders down so they last 12 months (even in forklift traffic) and can be taken up overnight. The company's Lead Team[4] typically handles these matters. We hope you have one.

The main thing is that borders get installed, from the ground up. I repeat myself when I say borders are the single most powerful visual device available for establishing and maintaining visual order. They accomplish even more than that. Let me illustrate with a story.

The Pattern of Work

As a consultant and coach in the field of workplace visuality, I am often asked to assess a company's level of visual competency. Some of these companies are well into their journey to visuality and know it; they want to know where to go deeper, how to go wider, and where "next" is.

Others think they are well on their way to completion but, based on my criteria, have barely started. Others have barely started. Still others are thinking about starting.

Over many years, I noticed that when I went to a company that either knew it had a long way to go—or had a long way to go but did not realize it—I would experience a genuine sense of panic in the first few moments after I walked onto the production floor. I couldn't figure out why. I mean I am good at what I do and, in my view, give terrific value to clients who want my help. Still I would feel panic; it was more than nervousness.

I would look out into the vast gray and brown (or white and blue) of their production floors, covered with machines, benches, and small clumps of people moving about, and a discourse would begin inside me that went something like this, "Oh my gosh, I haven't the foggiest idea what is going on this shop floor. I will

Automatic Recoil— The Visual Where in Action

Creating Visual Order that is Distinctive and Very Satisfying

In addition to remarkable cultural benefits, implementing visual order through an I-driven approach can produce a flood of visual inventions, even with elements as simple as borders, home addresses, and ID labels. The ones shown in this album are a sampling of what you can expect when you implement workplace visuality in your own company.

Rear-Headers Address ➤

Associates in the Rear Headers area at Trailmobile/Canada invented this superb home address announcing their department—installed directly into the production floor. Notice the person-width borders around the two workstations.

➤ **Double-Border Function at Harris**

Melody Sparrows at Harris Corp. (Quincy, IL) made sure that this red testing stand was always in visual order—whether she was using it (dashed border) or not (solid border). Brilliant visual detail!

◀ **Color Delivery Bands**

This Rolls-Royce factory in Britain is a feeder plant to many. While the facility works through its conversion to lean, visuality optimizes the current system. Each wide band of color in this splendid visual mini-system represents a delivery location, with the location name and associated part numbers listed on the wall, band by band.

Visual Creativity in the Details of Day-to-Day Work

The solutions in this album stand witness to individuals who are gaining control over their corners of the world through visual thinking. Their visual inventions don't just solve local challenges. They serve to drive organizational improvements deeper and deeper into the landscape of work.

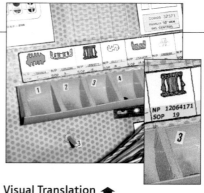

Photocopied Borders ▲

Bob Comeau, perhaps the first visual thinker ever at United Electric Controls (Boston), grew tired of outlining borders with markers, tape or paint. So he carried his tools over to the photocopy machine, laid them carefully on the glass, and hit the copy button for instant borders! In the solution you see here, he taped the borders down and covered them with Plexiglas. Better apply ID labels on those screwdrivers quick—they are beginning to look just like mine!

Visual Translation ▲

Notice the long part numbers (N/P) above each bin in this superb visual solution at the Delphi plant in Juarez, Mexico. The picture of the actual small part above each number translates it into something we can recognize at-a-glance. Associated SOPs are also noted by number.

◀ Color-Coded Gauges

Rick Ell, a formidable visual thinker at Parker Denison, developed this color-coded gauge drawer as part of a larger system he designed for the three products he machines and inspects in his area. Visit our website for a mini-case study on Rick's complete system (www.visualworkplace.com).

never be able to help these fine folks. Oh my gosh! What am I going to do? What am I going to say? This place is mayhem!"

This mental miasma, when it came, lasted only a nanosecond; still it was undeniably there, however fleetingly. Then I would mosey onto the floor, the cognitive flow would kick in, and I became a visual system expert again. Yet, the moment of miasma always struck me as odd, both in its recurrence and in its simple message of "Yikes!" Why did it always happen? What was it about?

The reason came to me at a seminar I was teaching in Texas. I was in the midst of explaining the importance of borders through the sequence of *visual where* solutions shown in Photo Album 10.

Here in the Incoming Inspection area at Parker Denison (formerly Denison Hydraulics, Marysville, Ohio), the team was repeatedly vexed by people putting overflow parts into the aisles—instead of making room for them in the designated location or finding a team member for help. Simple borders seemed to do nothing more than clarify this problem. Adding the big yellow X should have worked but just seemed to make people more creative about avoiding that as a solution. Only when the team painted the aisles solid yellow did the behavior change—and it changed instantly and forever. No one ever put overflow parts in the aisles again. Why?

No one got new training. No one was threatened or even reminded. The behavior simply changed from wrong to right. I had always written it off to the power of bright yellow paint. But at this particular seminar, people were pushing me for more. And then I remembered!

Twenty-five years earlier in New York City, I was in the process of trying (and failing) to still the noise in my head and meditate. I asked for help and the meditation instructor said this: *The mind is a pattern-seeking mechanism.* Huh? Twenty-five years later, at the Texas seminar, I understood.

The mind is a pattern-seeking mechanism. The mind will keep seeking the pattern until it finds one. And if it cannot find a pattern, it will continue seeking. That's what the mind does: It seeks patterns.

Most of us have experienced the mind's insistence upon finding pattern in our personal relationships. Your spouse is speaking to you with a great deal of animation; it is clear that he or she is trying to make a point, urgently. And you are trying to get the point. But you can't quite get the sounds coming out of her or his mouth to make sense. Your mind is seeking a pattern and drawing a blank. Finally, feeling nervous or very nervous, you say, "Honey, I really am trying. I can hear you. And I know it's important. But I can't seem to understand a word you are saying...."

Our mind will seek the pattern. But if it cannot find one, it goes into a mild level of stress. If the lack of pattern persists, the stress level rises. In extreme cases, the mind checks out (goes numb) or goes ballistic.

This is what people experience the first time they enter a new place, your factory for example. They may seem a bit distracted; but in reality, their minds are busily seeking a pattern, a place to hang their psychic hat—some way to link what is *new* and *unknown* with what is *familiar* and *known*.

When we lay down borders, we lay down the pattern of work. We lay down a certain physical logic of work for all to see, veterans and newcomers alike, visitors and owners. Those borders provide the pattern that the mind seeks and needs.

Newcomers can and will adapt to the absence of a pattern. It usually takes a week or two. During that period, they attempt to make sense out of their new work environment in the most physical, visual sense of the word. They need to I-dentify with their surroundings. Before the month is out, they are at ease. They have sought a pattern and either found one—or, in its absence, made one up so that the mind became satisfied.

In this way, people acquire a set of anchors and, even though an overarching, macro-pattern does not appear, they find that they can function pretty well on a micro-level—and do.

How different the first experience of the company would be if borders (the pattern) were already in place, waiting to greet newcomers with its message of sanity, safety, and stability.

From that day at the Texas seminar forward, I went onto the production floor and into offices prepared for mayhem, prepared to not be able to find a pattern (because there wasn't one), and from time to time I was happily disappointed.

Before moving to *Customer-Driven Visual Order* (the higher dimension of visual order), I want to remind you that one of the main purposes of workplace visuality is to make people think. There is benefit to gain, including larger profit margins, from getting people more fully engaged at work—mentally, emotionally, and physically. This was excellently illustrated, once again at Parker Denison, within the first year of the rollout. See Photo Album 12: *Right Angles Can Cause Motion* (located at the end of this chapter).

Photo Album 10

The Mind is a Pattern-Seeking Mechanism

Visual Thinking/Visual Order at Parker Denison (Marysville, OH)

There remains a lot to learn about how visual-information sharing works. Here is the sequence of solutions that taught me one of the great secrets of visuality's effectiveness.

Before ▶

This is the Incoming Inspection Department at Parker Denison before the launch of workplace visuality. Here we see the first attempt at orderliness. One of the chronic problems with this floor plan was that people outside the department kept putting overflow items into the area on either side of the material, blocking them, and blocking the aisles.

◀ **After (1)**

After learning about visual order, associates in the area laid down color-coded borders—orange for *incoming*, green for *outgoing* (top), and red for *hold*. While this helped the team tell status at-a-glance, people outside the department kept using the aisles for overflow. What to do?

After (2) ▶

Area associates decided to lay down big Xs in each aisle to send a "don't park here" message to others. But they were defeated once again. Cleverly, people outside the department found enough space for overflow boxes within each quadrant of the X—in the spaces left by the figure "X" itself. Drats, foiled again!

The Power of the Mind

Who knew that we humans respond with collective uniformity to the simple device of borders. But respond we do.

When we learn to think visually, we cannot help but notice visuality in the world around us. We see how visual devices in the community help us along our way and recognize when a needed device is missing.

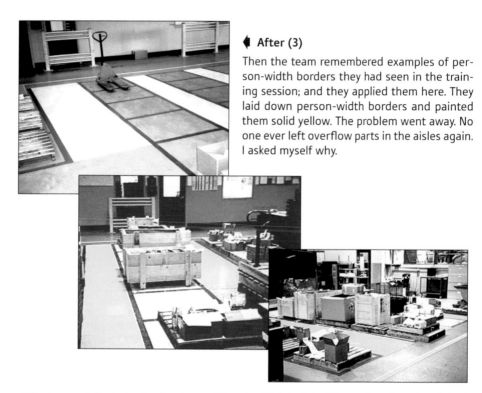

◀ After (3)

Then the team remembered examples of person-width borders they had seen in the training session; and they applied them here. They laid down person-width borders and painted them solid yellow. The problem went away. No one ever left overflow parts in the aisles again. I asked myself why.

What caused the behavior to change? People didn't just decide to obey the rules. It had to be something deeper, functioning on an esoteric or currently unseen level. Then I remembered! *The mind is a pattern-seeking mechanism.* The mind will look for a pattern until it finds one. Unknowingly, the inspection team had harnessed the power of the mind in favor of the standard it wanted upheld (see text for more).

As for this area, it stayed this way, fully visually-functional for nearly five years. Then the entire department was moved to another location in the facility.

Customer-Driven Visual Order

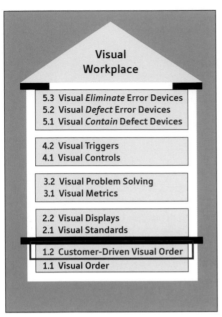

When associates succeed in addressing their need-to-know by thoroughly installing the visual answer to the where question, they gain compelling control over their corner of the world. As a result, they feel safe, in charge, and far more capable and confident of making in-process decisions than in the pre-visual workplace. Their "I" has begun to shine.

One of the remarkable by-products of this strengthened "I" is a shift of perspective from what-do-I-need-to-know to what-do-I-need-to-share. This is the unified I. We often hear this expressed as simply this: "How may I help you?"

Employees become service-minded. We see this in those who previously were Watchers and even more emphatically among those who were Grumblers. In a sense, the call to service becomes contagious in the department. Visual thinkers want to help; they want to be helpful. They are drawn to the needs of their co-workers, suppliers, and customers, both inside and external to the facility.

This shift inevitably leads people to become interested in visually answering the questions beyond "where?"—the other five core questions: What? When? Who? How Many? and How?

When they do, the workplace becomes populated with what is known as *Customer-Driven Visual Order.*

Still the domain of the value-add associate, customer-driven visual order deepens and widens visuality in the immediate work environment and catapults visual awareness in the area into the more advanced visual outcomes, the ones that exist on higher levels of the pathway: visual standards, visual displays, visual metrics, visual controls, and visual guarantees.

In theory, these advanced visual outcomes are created by employees other than line associates. But never mind; when such outcomes emerge as the result of visual thinking, they rightly get created by whomever is inspired to create them. They are, after all, simply the result of visual thinking.

As a result of implementing customer-driven visual order, anyone who visits the area, either external customer or supplier—or internal customer or suppliers (the area's upstream and downstream partners)—are bound to feel safer, smarter, and more connected to the goals and processes of that area. They too become aligned with that greater intent, the corporate will to excellence.

If you have already implemented your brand of 5S/industrial housekeeping/ workplace organization and the roll out seems stalled, call people's attention to customer-driven visual devices and mini-systems. Simply ask them to walk through their own area with the eyes of internal—and then external—customers and suppliers[5] and watch as a whole new crop of visual solutions get put in place.[6]

Photo Album 11 presents a set of first-rate customer-driven solutions, invented by value-add associates during a rollout of visual order.

With visual order—visuality's foundation—now fully in place, we move up the implementation pathway to visual standards, visual displays, visual metrics, and visual problem solving in the next chapter.

Photo Album 11

Customer-Driven-Visual Solutions

After we have visually satisfied our own need-to-know, we quite naturally turn to other people and ask how we may help. This produces an entire new crop of visual devices and mini-systems, this time focused on our need to share information—and thereby helping others become more successful in their own work. It is fitting, then, that the customer-driven devices you see in this album were the result of collaborative efforts between Strong I-s.

⬆ Customer-Driven Material Handling

Piet Mooren, a veteran welder at Royal Nooteboom Trailers (RNT/Holland), invented the very first customer-driven visual device in all of RNT, shown here. Piet wanted to make it easier for his colleague and material handler, Jean Heijink, to know what material was needed next without having to get off the forklift. So Piet made a magnetic plate that he wrote the part number on—in this case "2131." Low-cost/high-impact, the device worked!

◀ Customer-Driven Visual Metric.

Associates at Skyworks Solutions, a semi-conductor manufacturer near Boston, created this visual metric as part of customer-driven visual order.

Visual metrics are normally management's domain, but that did not stop this team. They advertised their personal best, along with their latest performance in order to highlight the importance of meeting the customer's required delivery time. Want to strengthen this metric? Add "Last Updated" information, the update frequency or interval, as well as a sector to capture the causes so the metric can drive improvement even harder.

Revitalizing Your 5S Rollout

After the addresses and labels are in place, many 5S initiatives fizzle out because people simply can't seem to think of what else they can make visual. Yet, most work environments offer a nearly limitless supply of information deficits and, therefore, a nearly limitless potential for visual devices and mini-systems that address those deficits. Revitalize your 5S initiative by helping people understand the need-to-share and by showing them lots and lots and lots of visual solutions, preferably from a wide array of industries outside of their own.

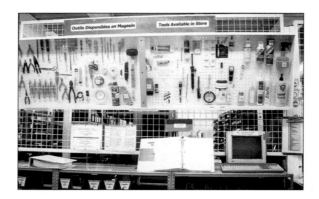

The Customer-Driven Store

When associates in charge of the company store at Harris Corp. in Montreal learned about customer-driven visual order, they already knew the question they wanted to make visual for their internal customers (fellow associates). They mounted all the most frequently-requested tools and gave each a number. Then co-workers simply asked for exactly what they needed and eliminated the back-and-forth that previously marred this simple transaction.

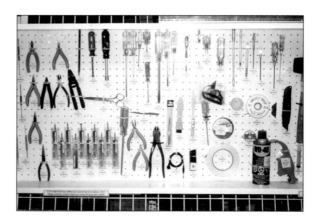

Photo Album 12

Right Angles Can Cause Motion

The Visual Evolution at Parker Denison

Parker Denison is a union shop (Marysville, OH) that produces high-precision hydraulic pumps. When the company committed to visual order, individuals and teams began to invent visual solutions that made the facility more visually compelling to customers and potential customers. It also created a level of employee engagement that the company had been seeking for decades.

One of the most important visual innovations in the company came from Bill Podolski and the other material movers. They saw that WIP pick-up/drop-off took them twice as long because borders were laid at right angles to the aisles. So the plant adopted angled (or slanty) borders—combined with person-width borders—as a new visual best practice.

▲ **Before**

They look beautiful but these right-angled borders actually caused motion!

▲ Bill's work on a forklift was made easy by slanty borders.

Chapter 5 Footnotes

1. For the fun of it and to force the issue, in a very literal sense, of the importance of working as a team, QMI will often institute the rule that, during the construction of the What-Is Map, a person can either hold a marker or a ruler for the drawing of the lines—but not both; so people have to work together. By the same token, a person can either wield a pair of scissors or a sticky note when cutting notes down to size. A bit contrived but it works!

2. Implementing borders in offices and other support areas requires an importantly different orientation. For the purposes of this book, we will illustrate border applications in the manufacturing setting.

3. *DuraStripe®* is a two-ply bordering product made of PVC and adhesive that requires no cure time to install (peel and stick) and can be removed by hand, with little or no residue; it stands up exceptionally well to fork-lift traffic, pallet jacks, and industrial floor scrubbers. See Resource Section for more.

4. In QMI's approach, the Lead Team is part of the company's on-site improvement infrastructure, formed as one of the implementation's startup requirements. See Startup Template in Appendix.

5. You can do this literally by arranging for your external customers (and then suppliers) to actually walk through a given department and tell the local team their needs-to-know. Then do the same for customers and suppliers, internal to the enterprise.

6. We have found that is imperative to show people actual examples of the devices in order to get them on board and creating ones of their own. We urge you to create or purchase excellent transfer materials that accomplish this. They are key to an effective launch and the subsequent long and rich life of every visual initiative. If you already have showcase level visuality in your facility, make sure to arrange for employees to regularly tour such areas. See Startup Template in Appendix.

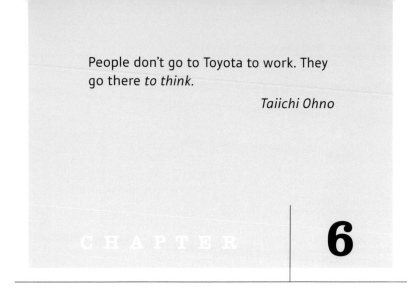

People don't go to Toyota to work. They go there *to think.*

Taiichi Ohno

Visual Standards, Displays, and Metrics

Remember the one simple reason why a visual workplace is required: People have too many questions. Some of these questions are asked but most of them are not—and when people don't ask the questions they need answers to, they make stuff up.

The non-visual enterprise is flooded with missing answers (information deficits); and where there are missing answers, there has got to be motion, moving without working. Lots of info deficits equals lots of motion.

As discussed in Chapter 5, on level one of the Pathway, value-add associates visually answer the first of the six core questions: Where? We implement visual order through the first of the visual workplace technologies: 5S+1. We install the *visual where* for everything that casts a shadow by applying borders, home addresses, and, as required, ID labels. Value-add employees lead this level of conversion through Doorway One in the Ten Doorway Framework.

When associates succeed in addressing their need-to-know through the visual

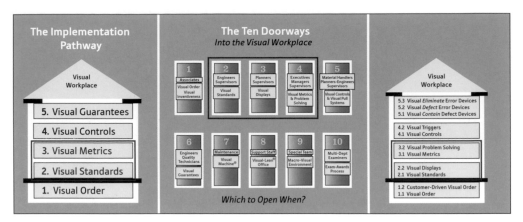

FIGURE 6.1:

DOORWAYS + LEVELS: STANDARDS, DISPLAYS, METRICS AND PROBLEM-SOLVING

answer to the *where* question, they naturally shift to their need-to-share and begin to visually answer the remaining five core questions (what, when, who, how many, and how). They do this under the banner of *customer-driven visual order*. When they do, they automatically cross the border into more advanced forms of workplace visuality.

Implementing these advanced visual functions is the focus of the remaining Pathway levels and the mandate of all other groups (other Doorways) in the organization. They are charged with installing the visual answers to the remaining five core questions, comprehensively across the enterprise.

Everyone in the enterprise makes a contribution to visuality in the workplace. Everyone must. The war against information deficits is impossible to win without participation from all organizational levels.

In this chapter, we present the next four visual methods, contained in the next two Pathway levels (Figure 6.1):

- Visual Standards   • Visual Metrics
- Visual Displays   • Visual Problem-Solving

These visual outcomes become the responsibility, variously, of supervisors, managers, engineers, and planners/schedulers to install. In no sense does this mean that line employees are barred from the process. On the contrary, area associates are regularly distinguished as major contributors to all of the above outcomes. Yet other groups must take the lead on the visual conversion process beyond visual order.[1] In parallel, associates continue their installation of the *visual where*, coached and supported by their supervisors and management.

Visual Standards (Level 2.1–Doorway 2)

The second of the ten doorways into the visual workplace is opened by supervisors and engineers, and targets *Visual Standards.*

However much line employees may contribute to making operational standards visual (and in some companies this can be considerable), visual standards are the principal domain of engineers and supervisors. Why? Because engineers and supervisors are held principally accountable for the precise performance of work—engineers in constructing appropriate standards, and supervisors in communicating them and overseeing their execution.

Standards define what is supposed to happen in the process of work, that which is planned and normal. Conversely, when standards are weak or simply fail, abnormalities result in the form of errors, mistakes, defects, rework, scrap, unplanned downtime, and associated late deliveries. Engineers and supervisors are expected, as part of their job, to identify and remedy related causes. In short, they are mandated to improve standards. Engineers and supervisors are very much the owners of this doorway.

Their challenge is to find ways to make technical and procedural information much more accessible and immediate by converting written specs and SOPs into a visual format.[2]

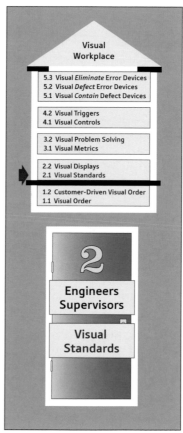

FIGURE 6.2:
VISUAL STANDARDS

This work is always best undertaken after visual order is launched and a semblance of location stability and predictability begins to emerge in the work environment. There is no sense publishing and promoting visual standards where the barest fundamentals of everyday work are still out of reach. As soon as visual order grabs and begins to create a sense of safety and stability in the area, supervisors can

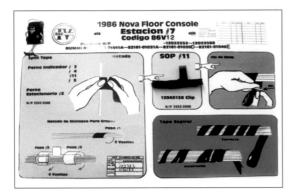

PHOTO 6.1:

TAPING STANDARD

This device, on the correct and incorrect way to tape a wiring harness, is posted on a clothes line directly over the assembly bench. (Delphi Automotive, Juarez, Mexico)

PHOTO 6.2:

ROOF FABRICATION STANDARDS

Notice the two 3-ring binders, each with a set of visual standards.
(Trailmobile/Canada, Toronto)

join with engineers and other technical staff to target the standards that need the most attention. Data on key performance indicators help in this focus—the details of quality, cost, delivery, and safety metrics.

The focus of visual standards is simply this: to capture technical and procedural standards (as defined in Chapter 2) in a visual format—and then to install these as close to the point of use as possible. Usually the process runs like this:

1. Simplify, focus, and reformat specification (attribute) information into a more visual and user-friendly format, along with precise information on standard operating procedures.

2. Include plenty of drawings and photos to illustrate key points. Remember: A picture is worth a 1000 words, so use photographs extensively as visual standards.

3. Laminate these (print out on card stock and apply thick laminate where possible).

4. Install relevant laminated cards at or very near the point of use:

   • On so-called *clothes lines* directly over work benches[3]

   • In plastic pockets that affix to the sides of work furniture and machines

   • On the spine of a 3-ring binder (without the covers), mounted at point of use (Photos 6.1 and 6.2)

One of the operative words here is "relevant"—because it is imperative that visual standards change frequently if they are to remain a useful and dynamic part of your improvement plan. Switch them out often as an intentional means of keeping the focus fresh. As with anything seen too frequently, visual standards can recede into the background like wall paper if they are not frequently replaced. This is more than a cosmetic consideration. When daily supervision is vitally connected to operator performance, performance will also improve because visual standards are handy. As this happens, improved performance in one area will point to new categories of problems and error in another, and new visual standards get pulled into place.

Even if you already ask people to keep a stack of laminated visual standards in a plastic pocket on the side of a bench or machine, find ways to help people easily spot, for example, this week's most critical standards—the ones that are still a bit shaky. Enterprising supervisors have been known to use garden flags, Christmas ornaments, flashing lights, and the like to draw people's attention to the critical few, those abnormalities that need to be addressed most urgently.

As you know from our discussion of the four types of visual devices in Chapter 1, visual standards have no power to change our behavior. Because they are a type of indicator, they simply tell us what to do; they cannot make us do it. The 30 mph speed limit sign by the side of the road is an example. It cannot make me slow down. I have to see it, understand it, and want to change my behavior. Otherwise, I simply blow by it. That's the nature of a visual standard. It provides vital detail to support excellent performance but cannot make us use that detail. (If you really want to help me adhere to the 30 mph speed limit, combine that visual indicator with a visual control—a speed bump or two. That'll slow me down!)

As with all visual indicators, visual standards depend for their effectiveness on people's willingness to comply and adhere. If you have implemented visual order effectively and laid down a useful visual and cultural foundation, your visual standards will have a measurable, even sizeable, impact on quality, cost, safety, and on-time delivery in every work area and, rolled up, across the company.

If you do not have the *visual where* and/or a cultural groundwork in place, you are likely to be disappointed—and may conclude that people just don't care.

Visual Displays (Level 2.2—Doorway 3)

Supervisors, managers, and schedulers own Doorway Three. Open it and you dis-

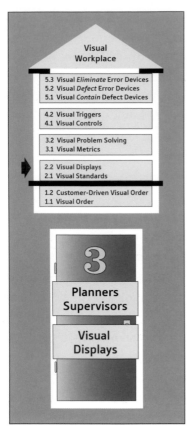

FIGURE 6.3:
VISUAL DISPLAYS (LEVEL 2.2)

cover *Visual Displays* and *Production Control Boards.*

Visual displays are the higher aspect or dimension of visual standards, capturing as they do the same range of visual answers to the core questions (where, what, when, who, how many, and how) as the previous doorway, but this time in a highly interactive format.

For companies making the transition from traditional to new manufacturing, visual displays are the glue that holds the company together while it reduces batch sizes and implements pull. In this, displays are indispensable.

Among their remarkable characteristics, visual displays are capable of holding vast amounts of interrelated information in real time, for all to see, enabling us to understand the status of a given situation in a single glance, make sound decisions, and confidently take timely, appropriate, and aligned action—either as an individual or as a team.

Those not well-acquainted with the superb functionality of visual displays may question why displays are needed at all. Some will point to the computer as the tool-of-choice, capable of sharing tons more information than a display, faster, and in ever-spiraling layers of complexity. And to this we say: Yes, we know; that is just the problem. (See photo 6.3)

The kind of information required to make sound decisions is information that has meaning, context, focus, and weight. Anyone who has ever worked with computer-based information has experienced the frequent and surprising fragmentation of information that computers can create in a nanosecond. When meaning devolves into data and data into minutia, it is often hard to get a picture big enough to take appropriate action. The resulting analysis/paralysis can choke the decision-making process.

With a visual display, the display owner co-locates the answers to his need-to-know questions on a single, interactive format. At times, this range is narrow as you see in Photo 6.4 (below). Other times, it can be extensive (Photo 6.5). In these and

all cases, a place is needed where related data can pool and influence each other so that the big picture—a snapshot of reality—can be seen.

Visual displays are not redundant in a world governed by computers. Instead, displays are the means by which we can, in real time, display data from multiple sources (including but not limited to the computer) and predict their discrete and multi-variant impact on the production flow. In this regard, for companies in transition, displays are powerful and unsurpassed in their usefulness.

While there are myriad exceptions, visual displays generally start from a supervisor's own personal need-to-know—and then, after a time, the need-to-share. Line supervisors struggle to keep track of literally dozens of data points that constantly change. These, in turn, trigger dozens of macro and micro decisions during the course of a single work shift: time to alert an upstream customer that the unit will arrive later than previously thought (or earlier); time to perform an unscheduled changeover in order to compensate for that; time to shift three assemblers over to the downstream operation where a bottleneck is beginning to form; gosh, the second shift cell leader is not going to make it in—stomach flu again.

Without a display that captures the latest set of data points in real time, supervisors, planners, and managers are in a constant state of alert and alarm because one or the other production element is, or is not, tipping in a favorable direction—and they have no idea which or when or how they should respond until it actually happens. They are out of control.

Supervisors are supposed to know everything. And yet they cannot. They are defeated before they even begin. Likewise, managers are supposed to know everything—and what they don't know, they turn to supervisors to supply. Especially in a traditional manufacturing setting, the truth is one of the most elusive elements of the work environment. Look as you might, you simply cannot find it. You may see it moving across the distant horizon, but as you move towards it, it changes or disappears.

PHOTO 6.4:

TOON AND HIS MATERIAL
DELIVERY DISPLAY

(ROYAL NOOTEBOOM TRAILERS, HOLLAND)

The visual workplace is about making the truth hold still long enough for us to see it, assess it, make a sound decision, and then take timely appropriate action. Nothing does this better than visual displays and production control boards. They are designed to provide snapshots of the truth across the spectrum of workplace concerns.

Although displays are exclusively focused, at first, on what the supervisor needs to know, from the outset they serve the interests of everyone.

Take, for example, Toon van Uden, who had been with Royal Nooteboom Trailers (RNT/Holland) for over 30 years and was one of some 25 supervisors and managers attending QMI's Visual Displays Workshop a few months after the launch of the visual rollout. RNT owner and then-president Henk Nooteboom announced at session's start that everyone there was expected to create and implement a visual display within three weeks of the workshop.

Toon, then chief supervisor of the Euro Trailer Line, decided he needed a display that answered one simple question: "Has the material I need for this order been delivered to the line?" (*ya* or *ne*, yes or no) (Photo 6.4). Toon drew some lines on a large sheet of paper, filled in the part numbers, and labeled two other columns: *ya* and *ne*. He then taped the sheet to a large standing shelf and was content. The only change he made over the next seven months before he retired was to mount the sheet on a board and screw the board on a tall standing shelf.

This display represented the extent of Toon's need-to-know and the questions that were uppermost in the worry part of his mind—did the material arrive yet? Yes? No?

By contrast, his colleague, Frank Mulder, chief supervisor of the company's *Magazin* or Store with 20 years at RNT under his belt, developed a splendid display (Photo 6.5), as interesting in its complexity as Toon's was in its simplicity. Frank needed to know everything. With 14 material handlers, inspectors, and store men working for him across two shifts, Frank could easily lose track of the detail. There came a time when keeping track of his staff became so complicated, Frank almost put in for a transfer.

Then he discovered visual displays and built one based on his over-riding need-

Each of the three panels on this display represents a week. Departments are listed and color-coded on the far left and next to them, the list of 13 area employees in yellow. Frank Mulder, display owner and chief supervisor of Stores, maps out tasks/people in 3-week blocks for everyone to know. (Royal Nooteboom Trailers, Holland)

FRANK MULDER   HENK HOP

to-know who was in today and what they were supposed to do. This display told him, three weeks out.

There are two points to keep in mind here. First, the display you see in Photo 6.5 did not look like that when Frank began. He started as Toon did with a sheet of paper and sticky notes. He made a first draft, tried it out, saw what worked and what didn't, listened for his own questions (his own need-to-know), and kept making refinements. He conferred with displays coordinator Henk Hop, who coached and lent insight into what a display should and could do; Henk kept moving Frank in the right direction.[4]

What was that direction? The single-focused (and some may say, "selfish") capture of Frank's need-to-know questions. Henk Hop made sure that Frank's visual solution was I-driven. As invariably happens with displays, when Frank had developed a display based on his personal need-to-know, the resultant device provided vital information to others because the answers were published in a centralized, highly visible, interactive format. The details of the displays changed as the truth changed. Splendid!

That's the way it goes with supervisors. When they know what's going on at-a-glance, thanks to a visual display, you know what's going on at-a-glance. This creates a tremendous sense of safety, sanity, and stability in the workplace—a condition more precious than gold. Why? Because those three conditions—safety, sanity, and stability—open up the possibility of unity. Unity redefines profit.

Before you move to the next Pathway level and associated Doorway, look at the visual displays in Photo Album 13.

Photo Album 13

Visual Displays and Production Control Boards

Information in an Interactive Format for All to See and Use

Visual displays are impressive in sharing complex information that changes often. In a lean plant, they are used to gain speed, transparency, and control over fast-moving processes—until process velocity exceeds the board's capacity to communicate. In traditional companies (hospitals, banks, engineering, and insurance firms included), displays address a wide range of communication challenges.

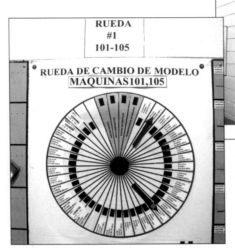

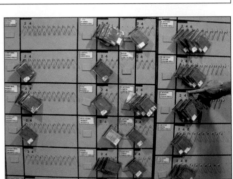

Linked Production & Changeover Displays ◄ ►

Two daily run-boards flank a third display in the shape of a wheel. The wheel display lists all the machines (and the parts each runs) in the area; Velcro arrows point to what's running now. The yellow sectors share machine maintenance information. (Deltronicos, Matamoras, Mexico)

Maintenance Work Order Display ►

This display, located in the main aisle of the plant, is Maintenance's way of letting everyone know (including maintenance personnel) what's been done (green), waiting to be done (yellow), and long overdue (red). (Delphi-Plant 20, Anderson, Indiana)

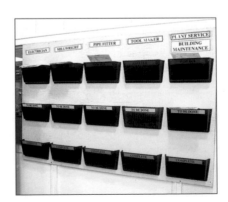

Keep Upgrading Your Display, Iteration after Iteration

All displays begin with the need-to-know of individuals looking for an easier way to get and give accurate, timely, and complete answers to recurrent questions. Do not expect to succeed with your first draft. Begin with sticky notes. Test it. Improve it. Then cycle through again. Rolls-Royce in Germany requires six upgrades before they consider a display in reasonable working order.

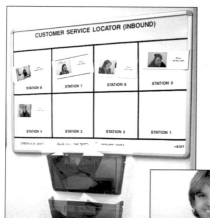

◀ "Who's on First" Display

Customer Service Supervisor Brenda Holetz designed this display to schedule customer service reps, practically all of whom work irregular shifts. Previously Brenda—and everyone else—kept checking and re-checking.

(Sears Product Repair Services, Sacramento, California)

BRENDA WITH
DRAFT ONE

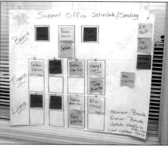

DRAFT TWO

◀ Complex Assembly Display

This meticulous production board at Rolls-Royce tracks complex subassemblies. Work order magnets move across bands of color—each representing a given operation or stage.

(Rolls-Royce, Oberursel, Germany)

Visual Metrics and Visual Problem-Solving

Doorway Four leads us to *Visual Metrics* and, its next linked step, *Visual Problem-Solving*. Supervisors, managers, and executives open this door and are responsible for what happens once inside.

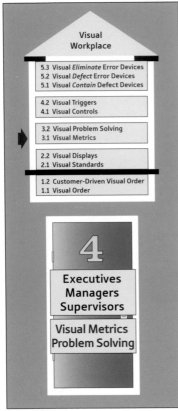

FIGURE 6.4:
VISUAL METRICS (LEVEL 3.1)

Visual Metrics (Level 3.1—Doorway 4)

The importance of measures is very much in the spotlight of late as organizations realize that feedback data are required as a baseline for problem solving. The Balanced Scorecard work of Kaplan and Norton[5] has been instrumental in driving home this point and helping companies construct a relevant set of metrics against a template of categories, such as Safety, Quality, Cost, Delivery, and Environment.

The measurement boards you see in Photo Album 14: *Metrics That Monitor Only* are of this type. While extraordinarily useful as a snapshot of current weekly and monthly conditions, such metrics are of limited use as improvement drivers. Though they are visual, they are not visual metrics.

Visual metrics do more than monitor performance and report back those data. They illuminate cause. Then, anchored in cause, they drive improvement activity down the causal chain until viable solutions are identified and installed. Used effectively, they do this relentlessly until breakthrough happens, the problem condition is eliminated, and the new improved condition is stabilized through visuality.

Though a visual metric is still a data point, a quantum, that provides feedback on a given performance and its outcome, its focus is unwavering on improving that performance and, as a result, its outcome. A visual metric never collects data unless those data are going to be used, immediately, to drive the metric in the direction of improvement—that is, unless action is going to be undertaken at once to improve those data.

This is a vital distinction in terms of outcome. Far too many companies, however, collect data just to analyze them, whether through Balanced Scorecard or some other technique. Managers will collect feedback and organize a response that may or may not happen immediately. When action is taken, many times it is merely to collect more data.

In such organizations, acting upon problematic data (measures) does not always happen—or if it happens, happens much later, sometimes weeks or months later. After all, the thinking seems to go, the problem is not going to go away by itself; if we wait a few weeks or months, it will still be there.

Visual metrics are different. For one thing, visual metrics are always in the voice of the user. Users are defined as persons or groups who own, cause, receive, and/or can solve the problem—not one of those but all of them. As a rule, abstract terms are avoided in favor of concrete, recognizable terms. Few people are motivated by percentage points or other abstractions. To be effective, a visual metric must speak in terms that are meaningful to any and all members of the user cluster.

Secondly, visual metrics are always tied to action; as soon as the data express an abnormality, people act to correct it. If there is an interval between knowledge and action, it is always as narrow as possible. Corrective action is undertaken immediately, at once.

Because of this "at once" requirement, a visual metric collects data at close intervals—every hour (hour after hour) or in 15-minute increments or exactly as the data occur. Daily data collection is not close enough for a visual metric, although areas accustomed to collecting weekly feedback may target daily data collection as their first stretch goal.

In addition, an effective visual metric will almost always provide internal points of comparison, usually in the form of *previous* versus *now* data—or *planned* versus *actual* data. Points of comparison allow us to notice a problem as it occurs and provide the start point for the pursuit of root cause.

That is another characteristic of a visual metric: It tracks and illuminates cause. As we will discuss in the visual problem-solving section (next), the notion of cause is fundamental to creating or improving standards—which, in actuality, is the true focus of problem-solving.

Finally, visual metrics are always posted prominently for all to see and consider.

The impact of all this is: Visual metrics are used to focus daily improvement efforts, track and illuminate cause, and drive further improvement.

Metrics That Monitor Only

Tracking Performance is Not the Same as Improving It

The measurement devices and displays in this album are used by many companies to display the results of their key performance indicators. Usually these are computer-generated, not easily read, and published weekly. We repeat: While extraordinarily useful as a snapshot of current weekly and monthly conditions, their use as improvement drivers is limited. Though they are visual, they are not visual metrics.

◀ Plantwide Metrics Board

This display is located on the site's main aisle so employees, customers, and other visitors can see it on their way to the production floor.
(Plymouth Tube, West Monroe, Louisiana)

Metrics Array ▶

Another proudly-presented set of performance metrics, these data show but do not drive performance indicators in this 3,000-person automotive supplier factory.
(Delphi Rimir, Matamoras, Mexico)

◀ Cell-Board

This cell-level measurement display provides team members with daily performance feedback, published weekly.
(Plymouth Tube, West Monroe, Louisiana)

See Photo Album 15: *Visual Metrics-Almost* for two measures that almost qualify as visual metrics and one that does not. The visual metric in Photo 6.6 is excellent, embodying all defining elements.

Who Owns the Metric?

Bear in mind who owns the metrics Doorway: executives, managers, and supervisors. In a traditional organization, these are the people responsible for designating what will be measured, when, and how. This is usually set in stone and collected religiously. No excuses. No deviations.

By contrast, in the new enterprise, leaders look for a different measurement framework: a linked and aligned set of global or corporate metrics that capture local equivalents on every level of the organizations. This is a crucial task since, recognized or not, each level of the organization has its own measurement voice.

Only if management knows this will it stand ready to help in the translation process. You may think you are doing a good job on linking measures companywide through your use of a Balanced Scorecard framework or the like. Yet the true test of a measurement system is whether the actual measures provide feedback that the people expected to carry out the improvement can identify with and call their own.

Yes, we are in the arena of policy-action deployment; and a thorough discussion of this is beyond the scope of this book. Suffice it to say, the organization's measurement approach is conceptualized and crafted in the boardroom and then cascaded down the enterprise. Senior managers must lead the way and the approach they choose will dictate the result.[6]

The visual metric shown in Photo 6.6 is among the best I have seen in some 25 years in the field.[7]

Created on the line at Deltronicos, a division of Delphi Automotive in Matamoros, Mexico, this visual metric collects data on quality defects in a radio assembly operation in hourly increments, across both shifts. But that's not all. Let's look.

- Brilliantly, it makes you segment or categorize the data by type as they are posted. The handful of defect types are abbreviated as URT, BR, CC, and so on. But there is more. This visual metric also pre-sets AQLs (Acceptable Quality Levels) in the process of data collection itself, including a double set of action trigger points—one for *alert* at the 3-defects level, and one for *take corrective action* at

Photo Album 15

Visual Metrics Drive Improvement

The first two metrics in this album embody some of the characteristics of an effective visual metric, but not all. The third metric is so large and visible that one might quickly assume it is a visual metric—but, most decidedly, it is not.

◀ Cell Metric

This visual metric is in a fast-paced machine cell. Note inclusion of the goal versus actual comparison points. (Wiremold, Connecticut)

Machine Metric ▶

This metric on a high-speed molding machine shows planned versus actual machine productivity as comparison points. The colored squares represent categories of known slow downs or stoppages, with sub-surface sensors that trigger the light in the appropriate box when one of these occurs. (Wiremold, Connecticut)

◀ Management Metric Only

This device is not a visual metric. Even though it tracks productivity, it does not drive improvement. And while it is big, bright, and easy-to-see, it lacks the required points of comparison (among other elements). Dating back to 1986, before computers took over the role, the device was made extra large so the numbers could be seen from a wide second-floor window where managers sat. (Packard Electric, Rio Bravo IV, Juarez, Mexico)

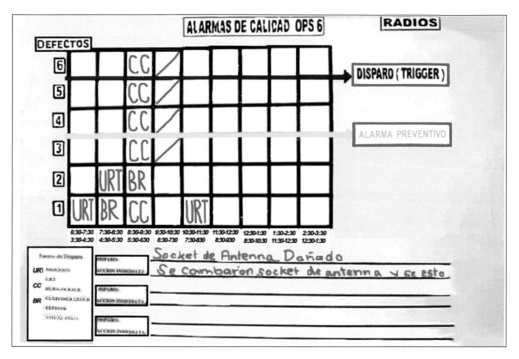

PHOTO 6.6:
SUPERB VISUAL METRIC AND IMPROVEMENT DRIVER
(DELTRONICOS, MATAMORAS, MEXICO)

the 5-defects level.

- If three defects of any type are posted in an hour, the yellow trigger line is activated and people become extra vigilant. If the number of defects (of any kind) hits five in the space of an hour, the line is shut down and immediate corrective action undertaken. The message is clear: Continuing to operate in the face of that degree of occurrence frequency without taking decisive corrective action would be risky.

- Finally, notice the area in the lower right-hand corner of the metrics board. It is a space where people can note actual or possible causes as each defect appears.

This Deltronicos metric has such a laser focus that it functions only a heart beat away from the next linked step. Let's look.

Visual Problem-Solving (Level 3.2—Doorway 4)

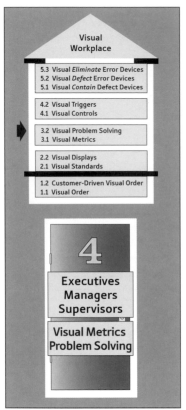

FIGURE 6.5:
VISUAL PROBLEM-SOLVING
(LEVEL 3.2)

Metrics that drive improvement—visual metrics—lead us directly to the next level on the Pathway to a visual workplace: *Visual Problem-Solving*.

Visual problem-solving is a structured sub-methodology, designed to minimize or eliminate the condition that your visual metric shows is off-the-mark. Most people equate such a condition to a problem. In fact, what we are looking at could be more accurately described as a weak standard—or no standard at all. Now that's a problem!

When a company expects operators (or managers, for that matter) to produce pre-set outcomes in the absence of published and easy-to-access standards, we are back to the make-stuff-up syndrome, symptomatic of an information-scarce work environment.

Early in my work in manufacturing and my research into the Toyota Production System, I realized that a reliable standard (an SOP) was and is simply a sequence of good causes. My simple equation goes: Good causes produce good effects. By the same token bad causes must produce bad effects—otherwise known as a problem. This understanding is so simple that there is danger that it can be overlooked completely. Yet, it is the doorway to excellence. Better causes mean better standards; better standards means better results.

Dr. Fukuda put me on the scent of this understanding one day at tea when he casually declared, in between sips, the following revolutionary definition of a standard:

> *A standard is made up of only those elements which, when not followed, result in a predictable defect or waste.*

I nearly dropped my teacup, stunned by the elegance and importance of this inverted definition. And it was this definition that proved instrumental in developing the logic of the visual workplace pathway. It subsequently led to the robust methodology for visual problem-solving that we address here in Level 3.2.

QMI calls this method the *ScoreBoard Process*. (You may already have a similar technique in your company's Improvement Tool Box.[8] Splendid!) The core elements of that process are:

1. Capture an array of good and bad causes on sticky notes and post on a highly-visible 3-D interactive format—a visual display.

2. Focus the process on the behavior or functioning of a visual metric, one capable of illuminating cause and driving the investigation down the causal chain.

3. Collect this metric in real time, in the shortest possible interval—not less than once a day, preferably hourly. Always include at least one point of comparison.

4. Segment the metric by cause or some other meaningful category, such as time or location.

5. Make sure that everyone and anyone can access and contribute to the display, equally and at will.

   Obvious exceptions apply. For example, problems of a confidential nature require the same visually interactive format but for the eyes of a selected few only.

6. Make a concerted commitment to involve all line employees, avoiding the representative elite approach.

7. Collect causes and generate improvement ideas non-selectively, with a bias for diversity.

8. Organize the format around discrete—even unique—cause elements, in lieu of highly generalized or homogeneous ones.

9. Operationalize the understanding that the success of this method depends on a high and on-going level of interactivity and engagement.

Remember that while this process may look as though we are solving a problem, in reality, we are defining and then improving a standard—a standard operating procedure. Once done, we stabilize the elements of the new or improved standard through further applications of visuality, ensuring that the outcome is sustainable. See Photo Album 16: *Visual Problem-Solving*.

Photo Album 16

Visual Problem-Solving

Solving Problems Permanently

Visual problem-solving shares weak standards openly so that all can participate in identifying causes and developing solutions. Consider laying out the problem in a large and an open format, posted directly in the area where the problem exists. This can go a long way to ensuring wide ownership of, and interest, in detailed causes and solutions that last.

◀ Visual Problem-Solving at RNT

This Visual ScoreBoard was posted directly on the production floor at Royal Nooteboom Trailers where employees added sticky notes at will. ➦

➦ Finding the Value in Inspection

Inspection can be said to be 100% non-value-adding (NVA); yet, it is a vital verification process for government contracts. When the inspection team at Pratt & Whitney (P&W) attacked NVA in the area, they meticulously tracked each work order, coupled with aggressive cause and solutions finding. (Pratt & Whitney, Connecticut)

COMPLETE VIEW OF THE
P&W PROCESS ➦

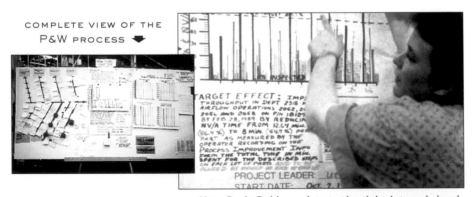

➦ Here Paula Robins points to the tight-interval visual metric that drove this process.

This concludes the discussion of these four levels of the Implementation Pathway and associated Doorways. In the next chapter, we look at the final levels as well as the Doorways that lead us to an enterprise-wide application of visual principles and outcomes. The journey continues.

Chapter 6 Footnotes

1. It goes without saying (doesn't it?) that all executives, managers, and supervisors implement visual order in their own value fields—in their own respective offices and in and on their respective desks. Requiring this group to install the *visual where* in these locations is not just a commitment to walking the talk; it is a major attack on motion on management levels that can positively impact the entire organization.

2. *Expert-OJT* provides software-based training and coaching services for developing software-based SOPs. See the Resource Section.

3. Use clothespins or binder clips to secure relevant visual SOPs in place, so that someone does not accidentally flip the card over to other standards when the current problem focus is on a specific one.

4. At Rolls-Royce in Oberursel, Germany, displays and control boards go through a required six upgrades before they are considered sufficiently effective. Even then, upgrades continue to be made as the informational layers of need-to-know and -share are widened and made more exact.

5. Robert S. Kaplan; David P. Norton, *The Balanced Scorecard: Translating Strategy into Action* (Harvard Business Press, MA, 1996).

6. For more on visual metrics, an aligned measurement approach, and the link with policy-action deployment (including the X-Type Matrix), watch for our upcoming book, *Visual Metrics: Doorway to an Aligned Workforce and Enterprise Excellence*. Also see Dr. Ryuji Fukuda's book, *Building Organizational Fitness: Management Methodology for Transformation and Strategic Advantage* (Productivity Press, 1997); and Dr. Tom Jackson's book, *Implementing a Lean Management System* (Productivity Press, 1996).

7. In this brief discussion of measurement systems, I cannot forego the opportunity of bringing your attention to the remarkable work of Dr. Thomas Johnson (Portland State University). See his *Profits Beyond Measure: Extraordinary Results Through Attention to Work and People* (The Free Press, 2000); and *Relevance Regained: From Top-Down Control to Bottom-Up Empowerment* (The Free Press, 1992).

8. Many such techniques reflect principles and elements of the brilliant CEDAC® methodology Dr. Fukuda developed in the 1970s. See his books, *Managerial Engineering* (Productivity Press, 1983); and *CEDAC: A Tool for Continuous Systematic Improvement* (Productivity Press, 1996).

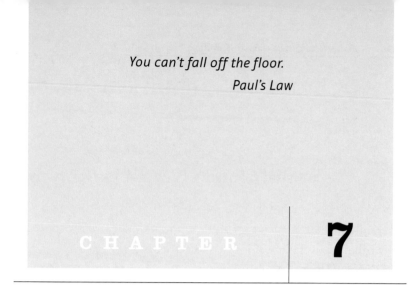

You can't fall off the floor.
Paul's Law

CHAPTER | **7**

Visual Controls, Guarantees, Machine, Office, and Beyond

As we move from visual metrics and problem-solving into the highest Pathway levels, the focus shifts to more powerful forms of information sharing, *Visual Controls* and *Visual Guarantees.* Their purpose is to install information more and more deeply into the landscape of work so that people can and must do the right thing.

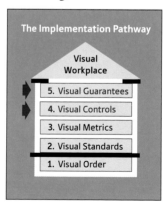

Devices on the control level and beyond don't bother to tell us what that right thing is. Nor do they attempt to clarify, motivate or influence. They simply make us do the right thing, with increasing surety—or prevent us from doing the wrong thing. Either way, they imbed adherence into the process of work itself and therein lies their extreme usefulness.

Visual controls[1], which further divide into controls

FIGURE 7.1

151

and pull systems, have significant power to restrict or limit behavior and control our choices. The only category of device more powerful is a visual guarantee which, at its most refined, eliminates the possibility of choice, entirely.

Visual Controls (Level 4.1—Doorway 5)

Low-cost/high impact visual controls are widely used in a visual workplace, implemented most often through value-add associates, with supervisors and technical staff often also making impressive contributions.

Visual controls structure size, number, range, and other quantifiable values into the physicality of the workplace in order to control behavior. In doing so, they visually answer the quantity-based core questions of how many or how much, and when or how long.

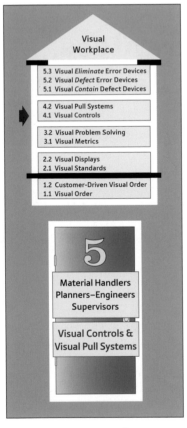

The structure explicit in a visual control constantly provides the exact information people need to continue adding value, whatever that value may be. Increasingly, visual controls focus on attribute level information, out-distancing the grosser forms of visual information found in borders, home addresses, and ID labels. Automatic recoil may form the foundation of workplace visuality—but it is visual controls that drive precision into performance.

Because the margin of personal choice becomes so narrow, visual controls require little or no interpretation. The device itself is the message. Here the link between visuality and the adage we quoted in Chapter 1 becomes inextricably linked: visuality, and more precisely visual controls, are key to helping people *do ordinary things extraordinarily well.*

Associates at Seton Identification Products, a catalogue company in Connecticut, implemented visual control solutions broadly in its fabrication and distribution areas. As with any effective visual device, these pretty much speak for themselves.

Photo 7.1 presents a visual safety control that

FIGURE 7.2

sends a clear message to stack bales of recycled cardboard up to the six-foot mark (emblazoned on the wall) and no further. Anything stacked above that control line has already proven dangerous. This mini-control system also includes a simple visual indicator that tells us to pull from the left.

The invention of visual controls is not as intuitive a process as devising more elementary forms of visuality. Training is needed so that people understand what controls are (and later guarantees) and how to devise them. On the other hand, if the workforce already has experience in implementing visual solutions progressively along the pathway, controls will seem to appear spontaneously. Don't be fooled. They are the result of visual thinking. (See Photo Album 17 for another Seton visual control.)

Strengthening Controls through Design-to-Task

Devices on the control level can be further enhanced by combining them with other principles in the visual paradigm. *Design-to-task* is one of the most powerful.

Design-to-task means physically co-locating things needed for a given task or operation. Tools are often the focal point (Photo 7.2).

Simply gather the tools needed for a particular operation in a specific location or container—a drawer, shelf, cart, cabinet or the like. Boldly designate a home for each item. Put the items in place (in their homes) and—presto-chango!—you can tell at-a-glance if everything you need to start and complete the task is in place—even if the task will take hours or even days. Try to insert an extra item that does not belong and it simply won't fit. That's the whole idea: to design the space and everything in it around a given task—design-to-task.

The principle of design-to-task can be applied to every work environment

PHOTO 7.2: DESIGN-TO-TASK TOOLS
Value-add associates at Parker Hannifin Aerospace (Irvine, CA) used to organize their tools on shadow boards. Now they use this outstanding design-to-task foam cutout system, oriented ergonomically. Notice how the yellow lining under the foam makes it easy to spot missing items, at-a-glance.

Photo Album 17

Visually Controlling Answers

A Window on Seton's Total Visual Conversion

Seton is a direct mail house, specializing in workplace identification products. In the late 1990s, Seton asked QMI to help implement workplace visuality, an especially fitting initiative. The result was spectacular by any measure, fueled by highly-creative employees on the value-add level and supportive, aligned managers.

CARLOS DELEON

ERIC JOHNSON

Eric Johnson and **Carlos DeLeon** in the Screen Department had to prepare enough silk screens during the day to keep the night shift supplied—anywhere from 42-52 screens. They spent a lot of time (motion) tallying up the screens throughout the day, once they located them, that is.

So they implemented the *visual where.* ➥

THE VISUAL WHERE

◀ While that helped, it did not end all motion. Many times a shift, Carlos and Eric were bent over counting how many screens were ready. So they invented the visual control to the left. That answered both questions—where and how many—in a single device. Splendid!

with repetitive work, most especially where pre-set protocols govern the delivery of value, such as in overhaul depots and hospitals. (See Photo Album 18 for other excellent design-to-task solutions.)

Visual Pull Systems (Level 4.2—Doorway 5)

Visual controls use structure (size and number) to share information. The result? We perform better. These devices can become even more powerful when linked with other visual controls and other operations, for example, material handling, replenishment, and flow.

When linked, they can trigger a chain of responses and produce a person/process/machine interface (demand-pull) that creates economies in all these dimensions. We call such a set of controls a *Visual Pull System*.

Min-Max Levels

At its most elementary, visible min/max (minimum-maximum) levels represent a simple visual pull system. Storage units marked to indicate the most amount of material allowed, as well as the restock level, makes it easy for us to tell at-a-glance when material is in full supply or running out, whether raw material, parts, medicine or paper clips (Photo 7.3).

The low-level mark triggers material handlers to replenish the supply. It pulls more into place, hence the term visual pull system.

Kanban

A more sophisticated visual pull system is kanban. Fundamentally, the concept of visual min/max levels applies in kanban as well, only this time the control elements link with the interests of the critical path or value

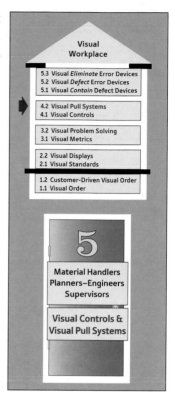

FIGURE 7.3

PHOTO 7.3:
MIN/MAX CONTROLS
Associates in final assembly put
this min-max control in place.
(Trailmobile/Canada)

Photo Album 18

Visually Controlling Tasks

Design-to-task is a crucial component of excellence in every work setting with repeated tasks, a powerful form of visual control.

Visual Controls + Design-to-Task

This outstanding foam-based design-to-task visual control was built into the top of a tool cart, and held tools and fixtures for a specific operation in LM-Aero's Tube Shop.
(Lockheed-Martin, Ft. Worth, Texas) ▶

Here the visually-controlled foam regulates and protects expensive parts as well the highly-specialized tools needed to assemble them. This complete delivery system is now the standard at all LM-Aero facilities and a Visual Best Practice. ▶

◀ Machinists at Rolls-Royce applied exactly the same visual principles to drawers. Works like a charm!
(Rolls-Royce, Oberursel, Germany)

Design-to-task is a critical visual principle at the Midwest Regional Medical Center (Chicago area) where the hospital pharmacy now prepares complete kits designed around specific emergency conditions.

stream[2] in highly repetitive production settings. Working together, visual information sharing and lean tools create the framework for an accelerated flow that can be controlled at will—that is, at the drumbeat, pleasure, and pull of the customer.

This is a lofty visual goal and an attainable one, no matter the industry.

Kanban is a physical card (or ticket) that visually signals the need for the delivery of raw material—or the need for transporting WIP or finished goods from one operation to another. Since these operations are always downstream, the dynamic of "pull" is achieved. Bins often replace cards, as in the well-known two-bin method, and can be equally effective.

Generally speaking, kanban and other demand-leveling approaches are most extensively used in the early and middle stages of a company's lean journey as a way to formulate, manage, and control the volume of production. Yet, because of its visual efficacy, these devices rarely disappear entirely as a production link, even when production speed increases dramatically and the distance between operations shrinks. They simply evolve.

In mixed-model environments, demand-flow devices often give way to high-speed *heijunka* systems, which schedule production and smooth out or manage order fluctuations linked to variety, batch size, timing, and sequence.

Heijunka (Japanese for "make flat and level") is a specific mechanism that segments the total volume of orders into scheduling intervals. Visually speaking, heijunka is a box that physically separates these intervals into time slots that will hold actual work orders (kanbans) in sequence.

For the limited purposes of this overview, understand that min/max levels, kanban, and heijunka are all visual pull systems and, as such, vital components of workplace visuality and the critical linking mechanisms that denote a visual-lean work environment. (See Photo Album 19 for more.)

Traffic-Light Pull

Kanban and heijunka are not the only visual pull systems available to a company. Another much admired visual method that incorporates pull principles uses traffic-light color coding to signal and control material delivery. This is a system so simple, its effectiveness continues to surprise.

We go to Matamoras, Mexico to the Delphi Rimir plant to visit the best system I have seen to date. At the time, Rimir supplied the auto industry with airbags, chiefly a cutting and sewing process.

An Assortment of Visual Pull Systems

This album includes classic and innovative kanban approaches, plus an extensive heijunka system.

Kanban & Heijunka

◄ Material handlers keep an eye on this 4-slot kanban square and replenish it before the last slot is empty.

High-volume production at Wiremold (CT) is kept on track through an extensive system of heijunka boxes. ◄

◄ About one in 12 men has some degree of color blindness (far less women). Because of that operators at Freudenberg-NOK (Cleveland, GA) invented a pull system, using animal fronts and backs (instead of color) to match kanban material with the right machines. The simpler you make a visual, the better. This one is modeled on the "Granimal" concept of kids matching the alligator shirt with alligator pants.

◄ Shown on left is a close up of one of the 350 individual heijunkas (above), the first scheduling level for the site.

◄ Each Wiremold cell has its own heijunka box to schedule, easing the way to smooth out work order fluctuations.

Photo 7.4 shows the central visual component of Rimir's material delivery system—the 3-color stack (simply a flat piece of wood, painted), resident in the first operation of the airbag process: cutting a roll of material into smaller sections for patterning.

How does this visual device work? Consider the stacked colors for a moment and it will come clear. Yes, that's right: When the material handler sees that the consumption of the roll material on this machine is getting close to the yellow mark, he knows that he must deliver a new roll soon.

At all costs, he must deliver the new roll before the current level hits the red—because at that point the machine will be out of material, have no new material to load, and need to shut down. This in turn will impact, if not stop, downstream operations that depend on cut material. Whether the enterprise is lean or not yet lean, unplanned stoppages of any kind spell trouble.

So that's how the Rimir device works and a very fine one it is. Wouldn't you agree? But did you know that this 3-color mechanism is the only one used for material delivery throughout the entire plant? That's right: a single device, repeated locally, for all material handling in every area throughout this 3000-person plant[3] (Photo Album 20).

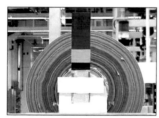

**PHOTO 7.4:
TRAFFIC-LIGHT
PULL DEVICE**

You may not have been a visual thinker when you first opened this book, but you are becoming one by now. So here's a question for you: Is the device you see in Photo 7.4 at the early stages of its application or is it mature? That is, was it installed a few weeks ago for the first time—or has it already gone through many iterations. What do you think the right answer is—and why do you think it? (You'll find the answer at the end of this chapter.)

Visual Guarantees (Level 5—Doorway 6)

In workplace visuality, the most refined form of information sharing is captured in the *Visual Guarantee* (*poka-yoke* system). It is also the most effective in accomplishing the goal of all workplace visuality: reliably and repeatedly helping us do the right thing—or avoid doing the wrong thing—in every workplace situation.

Assembly operations are an obvious venue for visual guarantees. Yet, as with all of workplace visuality, visual guarantees are powerful tools in any work setting, dis-

 **Photo Album 20**

Visual Material Handling
The Rimir system in this album demonstrates the power of keeping things simple as long as you also keep them visual.

Traffic-Light Pull

The red/yellow/green device appears on work stations throughout the Rimir value stream—even on the stacks of bobbins at individual sewing machines. One size fits all!

crete or continuous, across industries.

Guarantees fall into distinct categories or types, depending on the degree to which each device is able to ensure—guarantee—a performance outcome.[4] A closer

FIGURE 7.4

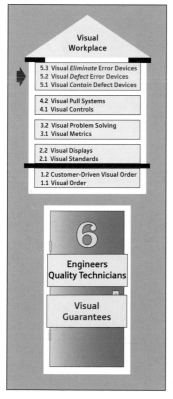

FIGURE 7.5

look shows us that, as with all visual devices, guarantees are also simply the visual answers to the six core questions, only on an extremely refined and minute level—on the level of attribute.

A visual guarantee translates specification information into the process of work itself. Actual devices range from plain mechanical apparatus to sensors and limit switches—all of them are ingenious.

Think of the gas pumps at your local service station. The pump itself is populated with an assortment of visual indicators, telling you the kind of gas, price, octane, credit cards accepted, as well as where to insert your card. On the level of specific action, however, the information disappears and the meaning becomes one with the performance of function.

Nowadays, for example, there are no instructions on how to properly put the gas pump back in its seat. Years ago, if you put the gas handle back the wrong way, gas could pour all over the asphalt. Visual guarantees were not yet an option. The problem of spills was addressed by prohibiting anyone but a trained attendant to pump gas. (See Photos 7.5 and 7.6)

Today, the design of the handle itself makes it impossible to re-seat the handle the wrong way. Short of not replacing the handle at all, there is only one way it goes into place and that is the right way. Whether you have been driving for thirty years and used to pumping your own gas, or just got your driver's license and are at the pump for the first time, you will put the gas handle back properly. You have no choice; and neither do I. It's visually guaranteed.[5]

The more effective a visual guarantee, the more

Visual Guarantee Masterpiece of Luis Catatao

Visual guarantees are point of use solutions that often impact the stream of value, directly. The one featured below is a *Type 3 Visual Guarantee*—it completely eliminates the possibility of the error that could lead to a defect.

Visual Guarantees

◀ The 28 bins in this rack at United Electric Controls (Watertown, MA) hold small parts for seven different switch and control assemblies. Because many of those small parts looked similar, operators made assembly mistakes that were only discovered in final test.

Value-add associate Luis Catatao was determined to find a way to put an end to those mistakes. ▶

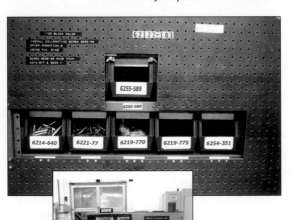

◀ Luis's solution was dazzling: a set of seven masking templates, one for each of the seven models. Each template had cut-outs for the bins with parts for a given model, only— making it impossible for an operator to access the wrong part.

◀ Rolls-Royce associates (Oberursel, Germany) saw Luis's invention at a QMI seminar and adapted it for a tricky machining process—requiring different sets of tips with very fine radii. Notice the second template in the foreground. (Visual inventiveness relies on people seeing lots of visual solutions from many industries.)

PHOTO 7.5:
YOUR FRIENDLY NEIGHBORHOOD
GAS PUMP, CIRCA 1957

PHOTO 7.6:
A MODERN GAS PUMP

deeply the information (the message) is imbedded in the item or process itself, so close to the point of use that the guarantee and the process or item are one.

That is exactly the point of visual guarantees. They remove choice so that we can only do the right thing. Doing the wrong thing is simply not an option. In a manner of speaking, a visual guarantee sets aside the human will and replaces it with one that is mechanical or electronic—and precisely aligned with the corporate intent. (See Photo Album 21.)

Doorway 6 Owner

The company's quality group owns the Doorway to visual guarantees; this group often works in concert with design and process engineers, and always with value-add associates. In fact, 70%-80% of the actual solutions result from interaction with production personnel.

The systematic implementation of visual guarantees usually happens late in the visual rollout, after the cultural foundation is firmly in place and most of the Doorways have been opened, to a greater or lesser extent.

If your company is hemorrhaging from quality problems, however, do not wait to begin until that visual/cultural foundation is in place. Hop the elevator to the top of the Pathway and attack your quality problems with the fierceness that threats to your survival warrant.

In the absence of threatening conditions, however, this phase of the visual rollout begins with quality personnel getting trained in visual guarantees and then training others. Intense learning, accompanied by plenty of trial and error, marks the first few application cycles. As local skill builds, so does the visual imagination. It is then only a matter of time before a core group becomes proficient in the method.

In most companies, quality assurance is eager to lead visual guarantee activity and to work with the very people (line employees) who, up to now, have worried about or dreaded QA's arrival in their area, like more bad news in a plague year. Instead, QA is welcomed as the hero it has become in elevating the process and the people who use it.

As in all robust implementations, creating visual guarantees is an iterative process with applications everywhere—in production, maintenance, material handling, supplier development, engineering, finance, and marketing—everywhere. The result? Defects are minimized, or even eliminated, to an extent previously unimaginable; and in the process, the workforce becomes masters of cause on the attribute level.

This is what Dr. Shigeo Shingo meant when he named Zero Quality Control (*poka-yoke* systems) as the goal of all quality activity. Eliminate the quality function entirely by building quality—perfection—into the process of work.[6]

Every enterprise interested in survival and sustainability at some stage resolves to implement visual guarantees as part of its strategic commitment to excellence. The return on this investment can be enormous.

• • • •

The Implementation Pathway to a visual workplace culminates on Level 5 with visual guarantees, but the Doorways continue.

There are four more, leading, on the one hand, to new application settings for already familiar visual methods—and, on the other, to new visual techniques and considerations.

Because this book is not an implementation manual, we overview the four remaining doorways rather than provide details on putting them in place.

The next two doorways are linked to specific workplace settings: Doorway 7 to the Visual Machine® and Doorway 8 to the Visual-Lean® Office.

Doorway 7: The Visual Machine®

Even though machines represent a company's most expensive asset, they are often taken for granted. The logic (or lack thereof) goes something like this: "Machines work—and when they don't work, call Maintenance. Machines break down. It can't be helped. That's all there is to it."

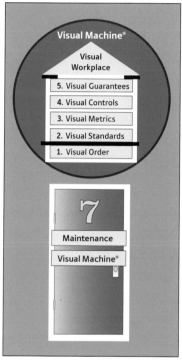

FIGURE 7.6

Similar notions apply to the time it takes to changeover and setup equipment for a new production run. There is a great deal a company can do—everyone can do—to improve machine effectiveness, changeover times, and equipment availability. One major component of this is the visual technology known as The Visual Machine®. The visual machine lets equipment speak.

In creating a visual machine, we install the full gamut of technologies and outcomes contained in the visual workplace pathway we have just walked through. The starting point may vary. For example, if you are faced with long changeovers (and to many, any changeover longer than ten minutes is considered excessive—yes, CNC machines included), let that be your initial focal point for making the machinery visual. (See Inset 7.1)

Then, when changeover times are viable, go back to Level 1 of the Pathway (the basement) and implement visual order on and around the machine and for all the fixtures, tools, and material locations that support your machine utilization. Then work your way up.

In our experience, there is nearly no end to the benefit you can create by applying visual principles to the machine environment. Positive outcomes abound. Where machine assets dominate, we suggest that those companies begin and anchor their enterprise-wide conversion to visuality exactly there.

Doorway 7 Owner

Maintenance owns Doorway 7. Much as we discussed with quality assurance and visual guarantees, Maintenance, in leading the visual machine initiative, can cast a

---

INSET 7.1: THE VISUAL MACHINE MEETS QCO AND TPM

Since the mid-1980s, thousands of companies around the world have found the flexibility and machine utilization they need to stay competitive by implementing Total Productive Maintenance (TPM) and Quick Changeover (QCO) methods.

The Visual Machine® uses visuality as the doorway to many of the same outstanding performance outcomes—with the added benefit that operators can get quickly and importantly involved from the very early stages.

Have you already launched TPM and QCO (I hope so)? Then use the principles and tools of the visual machine as a powerful complement to them.

In one company, setup took four hours or more on a 1,000-ton stamping press. Sixty days later, after the team applied QCO and the Visual Machine, the same setup took 1.5 hours. Six months after that, it was done in three minutes. That's not a typo! It does say "three minutes!"

In another company—this one with 5,000 screw machines—the best changeover anyone could achieve was an hour—and then on only 25% (1,250) of the machines; the rest took more, much more. Two years later, the best changeovers took 100 seconds or less—and on a startling 62% of the machines (3,100). And those are not typos either!

Astonishing? Yes. Unusual? Not anymore. Changeovers happen fast these days—at 80% to 90% of what they once were, thanks in great part to making the machine and all that supports it *visual.*

---

new role for itself in the enterprise, as well as a friendlier image.

Certainly there are many exceptions, yet in far too many organizations, maintenance technicians are burdened with the knowledge that if they don't keep the machines going, the company will fail and they, along with everyone else, will lose their jobs. And yet, they also know that the rest of the workforce represents the weakest link in a machine's overall effectiveness.

They know what you know: for example, that 60%-70% of all machine breakdowns are caused by mistakes in lubrication.

In the best of conditions, Maintenance has a daunting workload. In the worst, that workload can be demoralizing. When machine conditions are bad, everyone seems to be against maintainers. At the same time, maintainers may find they have to fight for everything—resources, time, you name it—and fight with everyone, sometimes even operators who, to them, often seem more skilled at causing breakdowns than preventing them. Faced with this, it is not hard to see why the maintenance crew sometimes has a reputation for being grumpy.

Imagine their jubilation when management commits to implementing the visual machine. In this simple, powerful approach, information vital to running, maintaining, changing over, and repairing equipment is visually installed directly in, on, and around the machinery itself. Through dozens of low-cost/high-impact visual devices and mini-systems, maintenance and operators alike can do what needs to be done in support of maximum machine availability—quickly, safely, and accurately. Here is a short list:

- Match-marks that help everyone and anyone see at-a-glance if bolts and slides are over tightened or loosening.

- Color-coded lubrication tags, lube diagrams, and lube cart so the right lubricant is used in the right quantity and at the right location.

- See-through red/yellow/green faces on temperature, speed, and pressure gauges so we can see at-a-glance if the machine is running normally or abnormally.

- Visual safety indicators and procedures on the machine at the exact point of use to reduce or even eliminate the possibility of risk.

- Visually ordered/color-coded material and tooling placement that make it easy for everyone and anyone to locate the correct WIP and dies for machine changeover.

Visual devices and mini-systems make machinery self-explaining so we can be self-regulating. They build common sense and a common improvement language directly into the physical work environment. The visual machine doesn't just help us do the right thing repeatedly, reliably and fast, it helps us prevent problems. (See Photo Album 22.)

In a world without visual devices and visual mini-systems, operators and maintainers alike are forced to rely on memory or costly trial-and-error to fill in for information deficits. The result? Long changeovers, long repair lead times, lost production, unhappy customers, and a demoralized workforce. Visual solutions put an end to all of that and refocus us on more advanced questions, such as: What is the highest level of equipment effectiveness and availability we can achieve?

Doorway 8: The Visual-Lean® Office

The excellence revolution had been around for more than decade before companies began to realize that the same principles and practices that were making the produc-

FIGURE 7.7

tion floor faster, better, and more profitable were applicable to other settings. Non-production functions also became targets for conversion. From there it was an easy step to seeking operational excellence in offices everywhere—hospitals, banks, retail stores, airports, at-home services, schools and colleges, and government agencies.

The knowledge content of workplace visuality is so universally relevant, it pertains to all work venues. If work is done there, visual principles and practices are bound to make as dramatic a positive impact as they do on the manufacturing floor.

At QMI, the method we use for improving these settings is the Visual-Lean® Office. Similar to visual machine applications, this implementation encompasses the gamut of pathway technologies and outcomes (Figure 7.7).

A Word about Office Implementations

After some trials and victories, I began to understand that while the knowledge base for achieving a visual office is identical to that of the shop floor, the implementation methodology is considerably different. A visual office conversion requires its own distinct set of application premises and practices if the outcome is to be comprehensive and sustainable.

The most powerful variable is linked to the difference in culture between most office and production environments. Consider these.

1. **People are used to groups.** People in offices are used to getting their work done in a group context, not in isolation from others. Working in groups, if not in teams, is the norm in office settings. This is not to say that the groups always work well, but there is a built-in tenet that office outputs are owned by the department.

   Unlike a production cell, it is difficult for the Finance Department to separate a financial report into its discrete components, the way one can with a sub-assembly. Even though many people may contribute to a report's various sections, the boundaries between those sections easily blur and ownership becomes a joint event.

2. **People own their work.** People in offices feel a greater sense of ownership over their jobs. They understand how pieces fit and recognize what they contribute to the whole much more readily than production personnel. By the same token, because individuals identify more closely with their work outputs, they often feel greater pride in their quality outputs and greater distress if their work is not up to standard.

   It has occurred to me more than once that the scope and focus of those who work in offices are more closely aligned to those of a good manager, often understanding the big picture and the purpose of their work, with great insight and appreciation.

3. **People are more self-supervising.** People in offices are used to more self-regulation. While they may require or even seek supervision on tasks, they rarely need or seek help on skill. The educational sequence that landed one person an office job is, more often than not, similar to (if not identical with) that of an office peer.

   For the most part, office personnel know what their job is and how to do it. Being micromanaged is a frequent complaint; people prefer instead an approach that "tells me what to do—not how to do it."

4. **People protect their territory.** Who hasn't heard offices called "small kingdoms?" That's usually said with some venom, but to me it makes sense. "Don't touch my desk" is my constant instruction around the office. I have a huge sense of ownership over my piles, and I respect that need in others.

   The fact is people in offices tend to be more protective of their work domains than production personnel. They do not like anyone messing with their value fields, their desks. It might as well be their purse or briefcase that's about to be transgressed. As things would have it, the habit of sharing one's desk with another is not widely practiced in the office community (not yet anyway)—whereas workbenches are commonly shared; they are rarely "owned."

Because of these considerations, QMI starts to implement workplace visuality in a manner that is substantially different from our startup approach on the shop floor. Although the telling details are beyond the scope of this book, let me clue you in on a few more of the most significant changes in our approach in offices.

For one thing, since time is the inventory of the office, we typically launch

Photo Album 22

Visual Machine—Visual Maintenance

The Visual Machine®

An implementation of the visual machine casts a wide net that can visually transform fixture and tooling protocols, lubrication and changeover practices, the maintenance function, and, of course, the machine itself.

Belts and pulleys are now in visual order on an un-used upper wall.

This machine is up and running, with two changeovers in queue.

The visual machine tells us what's normal.

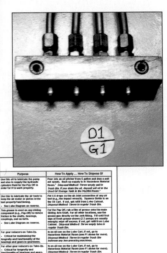

Quick changeover carts are visual carts.

Color-coded lubrication charts and lube discs minimize costly mistakes.

improvements to the value stream (lean) in close sequence to, sometimes in parallel with, the visual conversion. On the visual side, instead of waiting to implement the *visual where*, we use standards of visual practices, including the *visual where*, as an application pathway. Standards of office visuality drive the office initiative.

Yet there is also much that remains unchanged from our production floor implementation. For example, we never deviate from our commitment to create I-driven visuality. Nor do we lower our expectation that office personnel will invent remarkable, never-seen-before visual solutions.

Office personnel are as eager as anyone to self-solve their problems. In that regard, the vast majority of office personnel, including in hospitals, demonstrate a keen interest in seeing and understanding visual devices from all settings, including manufacturing. Anyone with a grasp of the eight building blocks will see past narrow details and extrapolate to their own needs. This is a hallmark of good visual thinking and commonplace among those who are properly trained in visual knowledge and know-how. (See Photo Album 23.)

• • • •

The final two Doorways (9 and 10) are not about a group of specific visual applications. Instead, they focus on linking up the organization and attaining a truly comprehensive outcome.

Especially in larger facilities or across several states, spreading visuality deeper, wider, and more quickly becomes a task requiring an unwavering focus as well as the means for integrating and standardizing a wide assortment of visual solutions. All this must be done without stifling the very creativity that has generated the local inventiveness at the heart of a series of Visual Best Practices.

Setting and implementing standards for workplace visuality are sizeable undertakings. The final two Doorways in QMI's approach to visual-information sharing recognizes this significant task and provides innovative new concepts, tools, and frameworks to address it.

Doorway 9: The Macro-Visual Environment

As a visual workplace initiative gathers speed (and by the eighth or ninth month it should), management will find itself faced with many micro decisions that, summed up, have a large impact on the macro environment. It is important to

Photo Album 23

The Visual-Lean® Office

Visual Inventiveness in the Office

Office visuality is vital to a company's pursuit of excellence, with office personnel eager and able to make so many inventive contributions.

➤ The executive who sits at this desk walks the talk.

➤ Full-disclosure helps everyone in this excellent customer-driven home address.

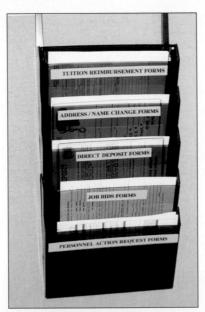

➤ Not just a forms holder—but one that speaks.

➤ No question about when the next pony express arrives.

Office Visuality

The visual component of the Visual-Lean® Office deploys a full range of visual technologies as seen in the offices of this Sears Product Repair Center. (Sacramento, CA)

◀ Customer-service value field: before and after.

◀ Every drawer has a table of contents.

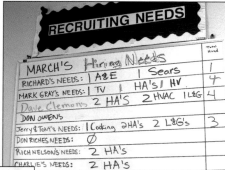

◀ Why keep hidden information that so many need to know?

HR took a ton of motion out of weekly orientation activity with this visually ordered supply cabinet. ▶

◀ This is the red-tag "corner."

FIGURE 7.8

form a special team to attend to them. That is precisely the purpose of the Macro-Visual Environment team.

This special team opens the ninth Doorway, the one that leads to standardizing and instituting such macro-visual mechanisms as:

- A coordinated color-coding system across multiple sites
- A network of visually integrated pull systems
- An array of visual links between all functions and across all sites
- An evolving framework of Visual Best Practices at each organizational level

Needless to say, those who serve on this macro team must be master visual thinkers themselves—*Visual Senseis*, in the popular parlance—able to identify not only minute and strategic forms of motion triggered by macro applications but also practiced in minimizing or even eliminating them through solutions that are visual.

Still, few organizations have developed a visual rollout sufficiently to reap the full benefit of this powerful team of in-house visual experts. This noted, however, do not conclude that a macro-visual team is warranted only in large or even multi-site organizations. On the contrary, macro needs start to surface as soon as more than one department begins its visual conversion, whether 200 people are involved or 20. At this early stage, it may be premature to expect this team to grasp the full implications of its purpose. It is no stretch to predict, however, that the team will learn a great deal through the doing, as long as they are well anchored in visual thinking concepts, principles, and examples—lots and lots examples.

The most important thing is to know enough to ask the right questions and recognize the right answers. A powerful tool in this is the Exam-Awards Process discussed next.

Doorway 10: The Exam-Awards Process

A large workforce and/or multiple sites create new sets of challenges when a company wants to implement a structured, sustainable approach to continuous improvement.

Doorway 10 opens to a comprehensive framework for rolling out visual stan-

FIGURE 7.9

dards across the enterprise, even as it continues to promote, recognize, and reward visual inventiveness and build individual and team leadership.

The cookie-cutter approach is death to workplace visuality. Visual devices and systems need the juice of local imaginations devising splendid solutions to problems that are often invisible to those outside the department.

No company can afford to give up that juice. It is crucial to sustainability and to solutions that really work.

For the past several years, QMI has been implementing a powerful framework called the Exam-Awards Process; we are amazed by the coherency and alignment it creates.

This final Doorway opens when senior management decides the site is ready for visual consolidation through a stepwise process—a series of exams. These exams are not designed to find fault or assess blame. Instead, they present a set of standards of practice that allows the workforce to understand what winning means in workplace visuality and how to implement accordingly. At the conclusion of an exam cycle, each department gets a score, based on the extent to which it succeeded (not failed) in implementing these standards.

Exams are administered by a set of cross-functional site examiners, preferably company volunteers, with highly educated visual eyesight and a deep desire to see visuality spread. They are I-driven, the company's visual leaders, and ace visual thinkers in their own right.

The exam questions are captured in a detailed set of visual scorecards that describes the visual requirements for the micro and macro work environments throughout the facility. In other words, they describe a corporate-wide set of criteria-based visual standards across all Pathway levels and Doorways.

Rolling out workplace visuality to a large site or multiple locations is not simply a matter of doing multiple applications of the same procedure. Scale makes its own demands. The level of specialized visual needs required in a large organizational environment runs roughly parallel to the scope and level of specialized information which that same organization routinely requires. Complex companies demand complex rollouts.

A robust implementation framework is required. It will take time to put this firmly in place as the core element of your sustainment process. Enterprise-wide visuality is capable of producing remarkable cost-savings along with work culture alignment. A company committed to excellence should seek—not shrink from—the highest possible level of visual integration and coherency.

With this, we conclude our treatment of the technologies of the visual workplace as discrete methods and outcomes. In the next and final chapter of this book, we will discuss their integration in a visual-lean alliance.

Answer to the question on page 159.

The device you see in Photo 7.4 is mature, having evolved over several years into the solution you see here.

How do we know? We know because, through visual thinking, we can "see" the psychology of the users—the operators themselves—and understand that they could never have tolerated a device like that at the start of its use.

Look at the bands of color. They tell the story: the wide green, the narrow yellow, and the almost non-existent red. They tell us that those who depend on this device for the delivery of the next needed roll are confident that it will show up in plenty of time.

So what did it look like in the beginning? We speculate it looked very much like the photo on the right, with its very wide band of red, starting even above where the green is now. "Yikes," it tells us, "bring me my next roll of material now! No, I do not want to wait! I want it where I can see it. Mine will not be the operation that shuts this facility down. I want my next roll NOW!"

The logic of workplace visuality is transparent.

A MATURE APPLICATION

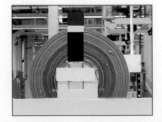

IN THE BEGINNING

Chapter 7 Footnotes

1 From time to time, people mistakenly refer to any visual device as a *visual control*. As explained in Chapter 1 in the Four Types of Visual Devices photo album, the term visual control is reserved for the category of visual devices that limits or restricts behavior, structurally, through size or number.

2 Despite anyone's thought to the contrary, in nearly 25 years in the field I have yet to find a single work setting that does not have repetitive work. Managers who declare otherwise do themselves and the people who look to them for leadership a grave disservice. And visual thinking artificially will stop with them.

3 Delphi Rimir has since replaced this 3-color system with a different material handling approach that better serves its pursuit of cost-savings. As with any powerfully driven enterprise, this plant has the openness, flexibility, strength, and resolve to constantly pursue the horizon called excellence. *Keep your eye on Delphi!*

4 There are three distinct levels of visual guarantees/poka-yoke devices: Type 1: Contains defects; Type 2: Detects errors as they occur; and Type 3: Eliminates the possibility of error.

5 Residents of New Jersey and Oregon cannot test this scenario because it is illegal for anyone but the gas station attendants to pump gas in those two states.

6 See Dr. Shingo's masterpiece, *Zero Quality Control: Source Inspection and the Poka-Yoke Systems* (Productivity Press, 1986), along with *Poka-Yoke: Improving Quality by Preventing Defects* (Productivity Press, 1988), Martin Hinckley's *Make No Mistake: An Outcome-Based Approach to Mistake-Proofing* (Productivity Press, 2001); and the poka-yoke work of Bruce Hamilton at The Greater Boston Manufacturing Partnership.

Section | Four

VISUAL-LEAN®

Now that you have acquainted yourself with the technologies of the visual workplace and the stunning cultural and bottom line benefits they produce, we step back and look at visuality as it expresses and supports that single mechanism for creating and delivering value—the enterprise.

In this next and final chapter, we make the case in favor of a visual-lean alliance, noting that these two powerful improvement strategies—visual and lean—become most effective when implemented in parallel, not one in the shadow of the other. Both are mighty and equal sources of dazzling enterprise-wide improvements.

Naturally, we position six sigma, theory of constraints, and the like with lean; they are all foremost methods for slicing the waste out of the value stream. Visual information sharing is a partner to them all.

No alliance artificially or arbitrarily separates one partner from the other. So a company should make no attempt to disconnect visual from its powerful technical allies. Nor should companies think of folding visuality into another method. To do so would rob the enterprise of a full visual victory.

Yet, in the face of the stunning success of the technical methods named above, an organization can overlook visuality's significant, substantial, and distinct contribution—by forgetting to implement it at all or implementing it in a cursory fashion only. When it does, the company not only constrains the gains, it inadvertently guarantees that technical benefits will erode in the absence of the sustainment that only visuality can provide.

The future ain't what it used to be.

Yogi Berra

The Visual-Lean® Alliance

Early in this book we declared that the visual workplace is not about buckets and brooms or posters and signs. We stated that workplace visuality is a compelling operational imperative, crucial to meeting daily performance goals, critical to greatly reduced lead times, and fundamental to an accelerated flow that you can control at will. It is the *language* of your production approach—whatever that may be—made visual. The richness and depth of this language depends upon the ability of your workforce to think visually.

In Chapter 1 we separated visual from lean by correctly naming them equally powerful, parallel strategies. The analogy used was the two wings of a bird. Neither is more important—both are equally important. Visual and lean are twin strategies. We spoke of the natural alliance between information and flow, meaning and pull.

Visual and lean share a single objective: to help the enterprise achieve excellence and ensure its long life and prosperity. Lean addresses the technical side of the equation, focusing on the surgical excision of macro-level waste and the relentless pursuit of the least-cost means. The result of an effective lean conversion, as we will discuss further below, is for lead times to shrink by 60%–80%—even more in many cases—and for productivity, quality levels, and market share to improve as dramatically and at that same time.

Visual is about information and people, targeting waste on a local or micro level. The technologies of the visual workplace translate information deficits into visual devices and systems that populate the work environment, enabling people to execute the standards formulated by lean into performance that is both precise and complete. Effectively and comprehensively implemented, workplace visuality does something more than simply enable lean outcomes. It makes them sustainable, allowing the organization to move from strength to strength. That sustainability is deeply rooted in visual's ability to engage the creativity of the workforce and capture it in concrete, functional form, liberating information—and in the process, the human will.

Visual takes on central business and cultural outcomes that lean does not and cannot address. Thus is the partnership between the two formed. The result of this alliance is an organization of vigor, focus, and longevity.

Have You Fully Utilized Visuality?

Achieving a visual workplace is no small task. It can take a company years to realize. Yet, at every step of the way—information deficit by information deficit, device by device—the work environment physically improves, as does quality, on-time delivery, safety, cost, employee morale, and customer satisfaction.

We have presented the pathway to this in a linear fashion—the technologies of the visual workplace and the associated ten Doorways—and spelled out the outcomes. We have showed you lots of examples of each.

While many companies have undertaken this change, few have truly completed it. Strangely, some companies will stop their forward march to visuality prematurely just because they have decided that the situation has so improved, further progress is not needed. Perhaps they just don't want to appear greedy or simply don't see the money left lying on the floor.

Others underestimate the distance they must cover or overestimate their progress thus far. Sometimes both. I am often asked to assess the level of competency and completion of a company's journey to workplace visuality, most often from organizations that already rank themselves high in visuality. Understandably, they seek the validation of an outside expert, as well as insight into where they could or should go next.

The assessment instrument I use is criteria-based, an adaptation of the implementation pathway presented in Section Three of this book. More often than not, however, the instrument never leaves my briefcase because the level of visuality is too elementary to warrant close scrutiny.

When asked to rank themselves on a scale of 1–10 (10 = high), most facilities proclaim themselves at eight, nine or even ten. In actuality, their visual rollouts are more on a level of three or four. While I have seen sites on a level six, I have yet to see an eight, based on this instrument.

There is no harm in valuing one's efforts highly. It is important to celebrate victories. Yet, it is equally important to understand the distance to the goal—and, most important, to see the goal itself, vividly, comprehensively, and in detail. Though vision is indispensable to the journey, achieving a visual workplace is not an act of faith. It is verifiable; it is quantifiable. It is a known outcome.

The visual workplace cannot be accomplished merely by tacking it onto to another powerful strategy—whether lean, six sigma, theory of constraints or what have you. Would you award a gold medal in figure skating to the winner of the decathlon just because he is a fine athlete and has a pair of figure skates in his closet?

We have returned once again to our theme: Visual is a powerful strategy in its own right. Do not assume that lean incorporates visual.[1] If you do, you will leave a tremendous amount of enterprise promise on the floor, gathering dust.

What Lean Contributes

Before we take a closer look at what is left lying on the floor, let's describe what lean brings to visual.

Without lean—without removing the barriers in the macro flow—gains produced by visual information sharing will never reach the bottom line. Instead, they will be absorbed by those barriers.

In one company that launched a full visual implementation, the welding department had documented a handsome 30% reduction in cell lead time. Yet, the benefit never showed up in increased throughput. Why? Because even though welding had time to spare, upstream processes—specifically material preparation—could not supply it with more orders, despite the company's three months of backlog.

By the same token, while downstream lines could have absorbed the increase—thanks to visual—the same bottleneck in material prep constrained their ability to produce more. Customer demand was strong (they were crying out for delivery)—but the macro process was not equipped to handle it.

The company badly needed a lean conversion. At my insistence, and I had to push very hard for it, management finally contracted with a lean implementation firm and began that part of the journey, even as it continued its visual rollout. Interestingly, the lean consultant was surprised at two things during his first visit: 1) that the bottlenecks were so severe; and 2) that the product flowed on a cell to cell level, nonetheless, once it was introduced into the value-add process.

He recognized that visuality had smoothed the way for a lean conversion. It had established flow. Only later did he also appreciate the way in which the visual rollout had prepared the workforce for the considerable challenges of converting to lean. The culture was ready, willing, and able to take lean on. All the push-back—the so-called resistance to change—had already transpired during the first stages of the visual initiative. The road not only opened before him, it rose up to meet him.

Visual needs lean as much as lean needs visual if the enterprise is to achieve excellence, live long, and prosper. That is the nature of alliance.

Now let's look at what lean, when implemented without visual, leaves lying on the floor.

What Visual Contributes

For over two decades, hundreds even thousands of companies have proven the benefits of lean. Lean success stories abound and they are formulaic, following an implementation protocol that is based on the world's understanding of the Toyota Production System,[2] arguably the finest system on the planet. Predictably splendid results will almost surely follow. The Shigeo Shingo Prize for Manufacturing Excellence sets forth this protocol with precision.[3]

Most of the world has translated the goals of TPS into, above and beyond everything else, an obsession with time—and therefore with its corollary, speed. Companies focus on removing as much time as possible from all processes that add value in the organization. They call this lean.[4]

The tight set of premises and considerations that have been connected with TPS, focus on relentless and deliberate elimination of waste, beginning with the waste of functional layouts.

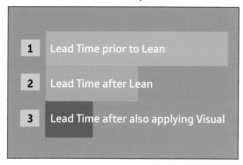

1 Lead Time prior to Lean

2 Lead Time after Lean

3 Lead Time after also applying Visual

FIGURE 8.1:
LEAD TIME REDUCTIONS, WITH
AND WITHOUT VISUALITY

As mentioned, an effective implementation of lean can reliably produce a 40% to 60% reduction in flow distance, flow time, utilized square footage—coupled with a 30% to 60% improvement in productivity, quality, on-time delivery, and safety. In some conversions, you can add 20% to the high end of both sets of percentages, sometimes even more.

Such results are splendid by any measure, and they provide the enterprise not only with enormous cost savings but also with the resources vital to stabilization or even growth and expansion. We celebrate this.

Yet what far too many of these successes overlook is, first, the fact that no mechanisms are in place to sustain those gains—and, second, that further substantial improvement gains are still available in what remains, but left unaddressed.

Setting aside for the moment that such gains will be difficult, if not impossible, to sustain without visuality, let's look at what lean does not touch. The following example uses average numbers (the range is often more dramatic but difficult to illustrate).

1. Acme Company is about to launch a lean conversion; the blue box in Figure 8.1 represents overall manufacturing lead time just before the launch.

2. The Acme Team applied lean tools iteratively and reduced overall lead time by 50% (the green box in Figure 8.1).

   The team applied an array of lean tools iteratively—five, six, even ten times, including 5S. The team pursued perfection, as Womack and Jones instruct.[5] They even implemented three six sigma projects that widened the success horizon further.

3. The team did not implement workplace visuality. If Acme had, even at this late

stage in the lean conversion, it could have reduced its overall manufacturing lead time further—on average another 50% (the red box in Figure 8.1).[6]

If you are not acquainted with the scope, power or process of workplace visuality, this may seem far-fetched. Yet for those companies who already know about the technologies of the visual workplace—and be assured that many do—they understand what visual can do and organize their conversion accordingly. They may implement visual and lean in parallel, or they may implement visual first and then lean. Or they may launch lean first, followed quickly by visual, but in any event they *will* implement both.

In so doing, they will build the bridge between flow and information and between pull and people. They will strengthen the natural partnership between lean and visual and make it a powerful alliance in the service of the entire enterprise. And there is another alliance of powerful proportions we need to discuss.

Critical-Path Visuals vs. Context Visuals

From the vantage point of 30,000 feet, we see that visual devices and systems can be divided into two distinct categories or classifications.

The first supports the value stream directly. Called *Critical-Path Visuals*, these devices define, reflect, and control the flow of work. The other set of visuals enhance and clarify the work environment itself, the space through which work flows. I call them *Context Visuals*.

By context visuals I refer to every solution you see in Chapter 5, both the ones that look ordinary and those that are outrageously inventive. Though the line often blurs, broadly speaking, critical path visuals are those seen in our discussion of kanban and other visual pull systems, including heijunka.

Which set is more important? Wrong question. Any attempt to favor one type of visuality over the other weakens the entire system and can result in a severe performance shortfall. Because we can never accurately assess the impact of the absence of a good, however, we can never know the benefit we failed to pursue. Our only choice is to wait until a competitor, who did embrace both, demonstrates the difference.

As with pitting the bottom-up against the top-down approach to power, we are fighting an empty battle. The enterprise needs both critical path visuals and context visuals, just as it needs command and control *and* empowerment. The alliance between context and critical-path visuals represents the collective intelligence—the consciousness—of the enterprise.

Critical-Path Visuals

Critical-path visual devices directly support the value stream. Their benefit is specific and predetermined. It is easy to track the business or cost benefit they produce. Critical-path visuals tangibly reduce lead time, improve quality, increase safety, and ensure better delivery times. If they cannot, they may be set aside as not relevant.

Let me say that again: Critical-path benefits are justifiable in advance.

Context Visuals

By contrast, context visuals require no such advanced vetting. Context visuals get implemented simply because they are part of the way the enterprise has decided it wants to conducts its business. In the world of lean conversions, context visuals are counter-intuitive. They cannot be reduced to a cost benefit, however much the organization may be impoverished without them.

Context visuality is a choice (though in our view not an option), implemented to create and then maintain, with certainty, a state of business readiness that is impossible to valuate.

This category of visuals establishes and preserves the logic of work, even in companies that have no plans to take on the journey to lean. The desire for work that makes sense is perhaps even more urgent in those venues, related as it is to our need for safety and stability.

Our belief in the world of work as well as our ability to perform erode when the workplace is unstable and unsafe. The underlying condition is fear. People don't like to admit it. You don't like to admit it, and I don't like to admit it. But in the absence of a sense of safety and sanity, there is fear. For value-add employees and their supervisors who are obliged to show up day after day after day, chronic instability at work (some may call it insanity) erodes the self as surely as it erodes profit.

Context visuals can put sanity and safety into an otherwise chaotic and fragmented workspace. (See Photo Albums 24 and 25.)

Sustainability

On a micro and macro level, workplace visuality is about sustainability. Unfortunately,

Critical-Path Visuals

Value Stream Visuals

Critical-path visuals define, anchor, and clarify the value-adding activity on a macro and micro level. Their benefits are, by definition, justifiable entirely in terms of cost, delivery, and quality.

Visuals Support Time-Based Objectives

You've seen all these critical-path visuals in earlier chapters, then as outcomes of specific visual technologies. As a visual rollout takes roots, such devices occur as a natural extension of visual thinking in support of time-based goals.

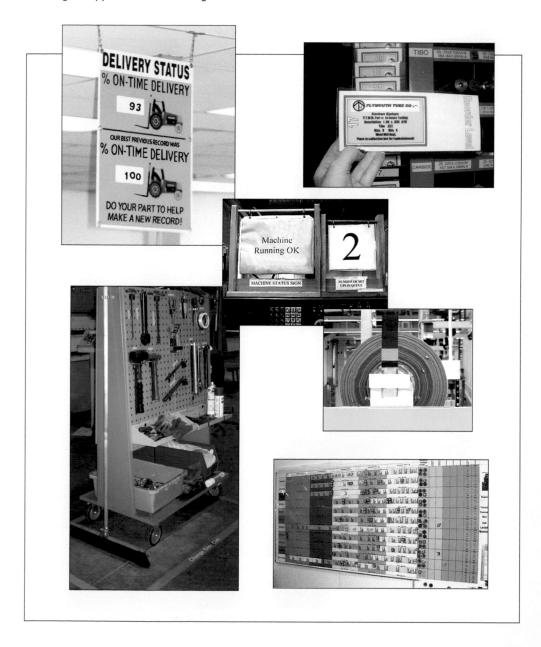

Photo Album 25

Context Visuals

Visuality that Creates the Context for Work

Not being able to valuate the cost-benefit of a visual device does not mean that it should not be implemented. Context visuals are like that—even though people may not be able to define the benefit of such devices with precision, they are certain they will be less productive without them.

Context Visuals Make Work Possible

Context visuals create a safe, sane, stable work environment and translate standards, imagination, and wisdom into concrete form. When enough context visuals are implemented, sustainment becomes a natural improvement outcome.

few companies have learned the importance of sustainability and that their hard-won gains will erode—and erode quickly—without visual information sharing. If they had realized this, they would have firmly committed to a visual rollout at the outset.

The most vivid example in my experience was a huge conglomerate that openly admitted to spending millions upon millions of dollars on a multi-site/multi-country lean conversion. The initial benefits were enormous and seemed to warrant the investment. Within three years, 40% to 60% of those gains began to erode. The past began to exert itself. The change was unsustainable.

It was at that time that we undertook a discussion of workplace visuality. The enterprise began to put visual devices and systems in place, specifically in order to regain the losses. Though much harder to implement as an afterthought, visual information sharing took its place in the improvement pantheon of that company, as an equal partner to lean.

How is it that, up to now, we have understood the matter of sustainability only in hindsight? We see this everywhere, including when we confer prizes for outstanding results. How different would our expectations be—as well as long-term results—if we did as Stephen Pollard, Chief Business Analyst at Rolls-Royce plc, suggests:

> *Confer an initial but temporary prize for excellent results. Then, putting great value on sustainability, check the company against the same criteria five years later, and if still warranted, confer the final and permanent prize.*

Why would he say that? Well for one thing, Steve is a huge advocate of workplace visuality. Go to his plants and you will see why. For another, his corporation has also faced gain erosion where visual technologies needed strengthening. Steve is a great believer in sustainment through visuality.

Yes, whatever the near-term results, time-based conversions are largely unsustainable without visuality. You already know the reasons for this. Implementing workplace visuality effectively creates the cultural alignment that is indispensable to authentic enterprise excellence. The simple act of implementing the *visual where* through value-add employees unlocks the pyramid of empowerment imbedded (we used the word imprisoned) in the traditional top-down model and triggers the inversion process. As I-driven visuality continues to be implemented, the inversion continues and completes.

As the visual workplace unfolds in your facility, context visuals begin to develop in parallel with the visuals of the critical path, and vice versa. They begin to inform and influence each other, and the lines between them blur. They strengthen each other.

A critical path visual that eluded an engineer is invented by a value-add associate who spotted a minute opportunity to anchor the value stream in his corner of the world. At the same time, your technical staff, previously fully occupied with defining and anchoring the value stream, suddenly sees the perfect opportunity to install the *visual where* in a previously overlooked detail of the path.

You have created a workforce of visual thinkers.

The Decision

In its fullness, an implementation of the visual workplace will change everything. Everything. In its fullness, it represents the creation of an entirely new set of competencies for people, process, and leadership.

To tell by looking. To tell everything by looking. To put an end to motion by liberating information that has long been imprisoned in the binders, reports, books, computer files, and data systems of the company—and in the hearts and minds of the workforce—and in the process to liberate the human will.

Lean inherited its need for speed and precision from Toyota. But Toyota is about more than just speed and precision. As with any genuinely world-class enterprise, adding value quickly (least-cost means) is always inextricably linked with culture. At Toyota, these are continually addressed in strong and equal measure, neither taking precedence over the other. Two wings of a bird.

To think or do otherwise is to deny the intent of the TPS system itself and shrink the possibility of the tremendous profit and alignment that are the promise of that strategy.

Many companies all over the world know this and organize their conversion pathways accordingly. Many have yet to learn. Those who already understand, implement visual and lean in parallel—information plus pull, with a focus on people development bridging the two.

Don't expect to make money off of your visual conversion. That is, don't do visual because it will make you money. Visual is not a money maker. It is a profit maker. Lean is the money maker, accelerating the flow and expanding your capacity for new business. Yet, if you do not implement visual, don't expect to keep the gains that lean provides. They will erode the way a cake dissolves in the rain.

If you are an executive, it will take courage, grit, and understanding to insist upon workplace visuality, especially in the face of the immediate and stunning results of a successful lean conversion. The visual workplace, with its foundation firmly set in people, leadership, and communication, represents a condition of business, not a forced march. It is the ground upon which the future of every enterprise rests.

The decision is yours.

Chapter 8 Footnotes

1. As previously mentioned, the teaching of lean principles and tools always includes a module on 5S/industrial housekeeping/workplace organization. As a rule, this content is cursory at best, usually delivered in less than an hour. Major emphasis is on getting rid of the junk (a good idea in every setting), with some time and instruction spent on those visual applications that promote orderliness—lines and labels, as they are called.

   Generally speaking, 5S taught within a lean curriculum can produce a type of cookie-cutter response that rarely touches the depth and inventiveness true visuality can and must trigger.

   Considering the content in this book's previous chapters, it should now be clear why we cannot consider such instruction equivalent to introducing, let alone teaching, workplace visuality.

   Lean does not incorporate workplace visuality.

2. Over the years, students of Toyota and its production system (TPS) have attempted to describe a definitive set of principles and components of that system. Yet, as with all dynamic, living events, TPS continually eludes final definition. It is always evolving.

   The extent to which this is true was brought home to me when I visited a company in Mexico several years ago. The organization had already mastered the elements of TPS as widely understood by North American practitioners. Quick changeovers, one-piece flow, and cellular design were solidly in place, with all the attendant dramatic reductions in lead time, throughput, productivity, accidents, defects, and, of course, costs.

   It was a jewel of a system, and one that was replicated throughout the dozens of plants in the corporation.

   Then the head of the corporation issued a mandate for each site to seek and find a new level of improvement—a breakthrough level. The TPS deck, so to speak, was thrown into the air, and when the cards came down, things had radically changed.

   This was about the time of my visit. I saw a plant that had just increased throughout and productivity by 30% by de-coupling its previously takt-time driven cells. Well and closely held beliefs about how TPS should run had been thrown out the window. This was a TPS I had never seen.

   The facility had turned its back on one-piece flow. De-coupled value fields (cells) were laid out in assembly lines again. The result again: a 30% increase in productivity and throughput, with no diminishment in previous quality or on-time delivery levels.

   I sat down. How could this be: a complete contradiction of fundamental TPS principles and a reversion to the past? Then I realized that TPS is nothing if it is not alive, vital, robust, and always seeking its next breakthrough.

   TPS has no artificial allegiance to itself or anything else, including what others may think TPS is about. Toyota is not in the business of implementing TPS. It is in the business of discovering what it needs to gain greater stability, expansion, and prosperity. And in this it succeeds with remarkable predictability.

3. Hailed the "Nobel Prize of Manufacturing" by *Business Week*, the Shigeo Shingo Prize for Manufacturing is named after the co-architect of the Toyota Production System, Dr. Shigeo Shingo. Any organization seeking insight into TPS and its implementation should study the Shingo Prize criteria. See the Resource Section of this book for more on this outstanding national process.

4. Since speed is a corollary of time, the obsession with time sometimes warps into an obsession with speed. But lean does not mean producing as fast as you can.

5. James P. Womack and Daniel T. Jones, *Lean Thinking: Banish Waste* and *Create Wealth in Your Corporation* (Simon & Shuster, 1996).

6. Percentages vary from one company to the next, with some results greater while others less, depending on a host of factors.

APPENDIX

List of Figures, Photos, Albums, and Insets

Chapter 1: The Visual Workplace and the Excellent Enterprise

Figure 1.1   Wings of a Bird, 9

Photo Album 1   Visual Where at Fleet Engineers, 12

Photo Album 2   Building Adherence through Visuality, 14

Figure 1.2   Well-Intentioned "I", 16

Figure 1.3   Bunch of "I-s", 17

Figure 1.4   Alignment, 17

Photo Album 3   Creating a Workforce of Visual Thinkers at RNT, 18-19

Chapter 2: The Building Blocks of Visual Thinking

Figure 2.1   Eight Building Blocks, 23

Figure 2.2   Need-To-Know and Need-To-Share, 24

Inset 2.1   Need-To-Know, 25

Figure 2.3   What Do I Need to Know, 28

Inset 2.2   Need-To-Share, 29

Figure 2.4   What Do I Need to Share?, 29

Inset 2.3   Definition of a Visual Workplace, 31

Inset 2.4   What is a Technical Standard?, 31

Inset 2.5   What is a Procedural Standard?, 32

Inset 2.6   ISO and Workplace Visuality—When & Why, 33

Photo Album 4   Six Core Questions Made Visual, 34-35

Figure 2.5   Six Core Questions, 36

Inset 2.7   First-Question-Is-Free Rule, 37

Figure 2.6   Forms of Motion, 38

Inset: 2.8   What Motion is Not, 39

Inset 2.9   Eight Deadly Wastes Versus Motion, 41

Inset 2.10   Information Hoarders-Information Czars, 42

Photo 2.1   Bonding Department Before, 45

Photo 2.2   Paulette Benedictus, 47

Figure 2.7   Cycle of Visual Thinking, 49

Photo Album 5   Making the Value Field Visual, 50-51

Chapter 3: Leadership and the Power Inversion

Figure 3.2   Top-Down Paradigm, 58

Figure 3.3   Bottom-Up Paradigm, 58

Figure 3.4   Different Functions-Different Groups, 60

Figure 3.5   Resolution of Opposites, 60

Figure 3.6   Ancient Symbol of Unity, 61

Figure 3.7   Geography of Common Ground, 61

Figure 3.8   Caught in the Middle, 63

Figure 3.9   Top-Down Pyramid, 65

Figure 3.10   Separation + Inversion of the Bottom-Up Pyramid, 66

Figure 3.11   Two Pyramids Approach and Blend, 67

Figure 3.12   Need-To-Know, 72

Photo Case Study   Angie Alvarado: The Visual Truck, 73-77

Chapter 4: The I-Driven Culture

Inset 4.1   Evolution of the I", 85

Figure 4.1   Yet Another Form of the Dominance Hierarchy, 87

Photo Album 6   Visual Inventiveness at United Electric, 90-91

Figure 4.2   Phase 1-Shift from Weak-I to Strong-I, 92

Figure 4.3   Phase 2-Shift from Strong-I to Unified-I, 93

Figure 4.4   Evolution of the "I" (both phases), 94

Photo Album 7   Kanban and Visual Inventiveness, 96

Chapter 5: Visual Order: Visuality's Foundation

Figure 5.1   Visual Order (Level 1.1-Doorway 1), 102

Figure 5.2   5S+1-Visual Order, 103

Figure 5.3   Sort Through/Sort Out, 105

Figure 5.4   Scrub + Secure Safety + Select Locations, 107

Inset 5.1   Executives and Managers-Keepers of the Flame, 108-109

Figure 5.5   What-Is Map (artist rendering), 111

Figure 5.6   Dream Map, 111

Photo Album 8   S2 + S3 Solutions at Trailmobile/Canada, 112-113

Photo Album 9   Automatic Recoil-Visual Where in Action, 116-117

Photo Album 10   Mind is a Pattern-Seeking Mechanism, 120-121

Figure 5.7   Customer-Driven Visual Order (Level 1.2), 122

Photo Album 11   Customer-Driven-Visual Solutions, 124-125

Photo Album 12   Right Angles Can Cause Motion, 126

Chapter 6: Visual Standards, Displays, and Visual Metrics

Figure 6.1   Doorways + Levels: Standards, Displays, Metrics and
                    Problem-Solving, 130

Figure 6.2   Visual Standards (Level 2.1-Doorway 2), 131

Photo 6.1   Taping Standard, 132

Photo 6.2   Roof Fabrication Standards, 132

Figure 6.3   Visual Displays (Level 2.2-Doorway 3), 134

Photo 6.3   Hotel Display, 135

Photo 6.4   Toon and His Material Delivery Display, 136

Photo 6.5   Visual Display in Stores, 137

Figure 6.4:   Visual Metrics (Level 3.1-Doorway 4), 138

Photo Album 13   Visual Displays and Production Control Boards, 140-141

Photo Album 14   Metrics That Only Monitor, 142

Photo 6.6   Superb Visual Metric and Improvement Driver, 144

Figure 6.5   Visual Problem-Solving (Level 3.2-Doorway 4), 146

Photo Album 15   Visual Metrics Almost, 146

Photo Album 16   Visual Problem-Solving, 148

Chapter 7: Visual Controls, Guarantees, Machine, Office, and Beyond

Figure 7.1   Pathway: Controls and Guarantees, 151

Figure 7.2   Pathway: Visual Controls (Level 4.1-Doorway 5), 152

Photo 7.1   Safety Visual Control, 153

Photo 7.2   Design-to-Task Tools, 153

Photo Album 17   Visually Controlling Answers, 154

Figure 7.3   Visual Pull Systems (Level 4.2-Doorway 5), 155

Photo 7.3   Min/Max Controls, 155

Photo Album 18   Visual Controls + Design-to-Task, 156

Photo Album 19   Kanban & Heijunka, 158

Photo 7.4   Traffic-Light Pull Device, 159

Photo Album 20   Traffic-Light Pull, 160

Figure 7.4   Visual Guarantees (Level 5), 161

Figure 7.5   Three Types of Guarantees (Doorway 6), 161

Photo Album 21   Visual Guarantees, 162

Photo 7.5   Your Friendly Neighborhood Gas Pump, Circa 1957, 163

Photo 7.6   A Modern Gas Pump, 163

Figure 7.6   Visual Machine (Doorway 7), 165

Inset 7.1   Visual Machine Meets QCO and TPM, 166

Figure 7.7   Visual Office (Doorway 8), 168

Photo Album 22   Visual Machine-Visual Maintenance, 170

Photo Album 23   Visual Office, 172-173

Figure 7.8   Macro-Visual Environment (Doorway 9), 174

Figure 7.9   Exam-Awards Process (Doorway 10), 175

Chapter 8: The Visual-Lean Alliance

Figure 8.1   Lead Time Reductions, With and Without Visuality, 185

Photo Album 24   Critical-Path Visuals, 188-189

Photo Album 25   Context Visuals, 190-191

The Six Startup Requirements
QMI's Template for Preparing for an
Effective Implementation

The field of manufacturing improvement is strewn with broken dreams and progress that might have been (but never was). All too many companies behave as though just thinking about "a change for the better" will make it so. Nothing could be farther from reality. For improvement to happen, certain conditions or requirements must be met from the outset. If they are not, the effort fails *and* we seldom realize why.

Over the years, QMI has discovered that when the following six elements are in place at the outset of an implementation, the likelihood of success rises exponentially.

1. Vision

2. Systematic Methodology

3. Excellent Transfer Materials

4. On-site Leadership: The 3-Legged Stool

5. Focus: Use of the Laminated Map

6. Resolve at the Top: An Official Improvement Time Policy

One: A Clear, Attainable Vision. Vision comes first, then transformation. Even though you may have never experienced a comprehensive visual workplace first hand, you have visited places where what was supposed to happen did happen because of visual devices—and it happened remarkably well. Before you (or anyone else) begin the visual journey, choose a location that can serve as your vision place—your touchstone for inspiration—until you have created one within your own company. Think of MacDonald's, the airport, local library, multiplex cinema, office supply store or, my favorite, Disneyland.

Two: Systematic Methodology. Vision without a step-by-step implementation roadmap is only a hope. Select a robust and orderly improvement method that has produced proven, measurable results, follow it carefully for one to three implementation cycles, and then, after you have understood it and your unique local needs, adapt it and make it your own.

Three: Excellent Transfer Materials. How will you transfer vision, knowledge, know-how, and excitement to others? You need a materials package that includes:

- Excellent, proven materials that teach a systematic methodology—including concepts, principles, models, frameworks, tools, and application exercises.

- Scores (if not hundreds) of splendid photos of visual solutions and explanations—not just from your industry but from many industries.

Outstanding instructional materials are indispensable to learning and, therefore, to change.

Four: On-Site Leadership. Company conversions do not happen overnight, not if the gains are to endure. To lead a visual transformation, you need a small team of high-functioning, emotionally-sturdy individuals who are willing and able to be held accountable for the progress of the rollout, in terms of both improvement in the work culture and in the bottom-line.

These will be valued members of the workforce. In a QMI implementation, we always ask the client company to designate: a management champion (highest ranking site executive), a project manager (called the Visual Workplace Coordinator), and a Lead Team, a small group of hands-on supporters (peers) to assist the coordinator in the many logistical and administrative tasks that every successful rollout requires.

Later in the implementation, volunteers are invited from the value-add level to serve on a Visual Workplace Steering Team; this group is the eyes and ears of the production floor and an invaluable help in helping management keep the implementation on track and productive.

Five: Focus through the Laminated Map. One of the early problems in a conversion happens when management bites off more than it can chew. Typically, this means a decision was made to rollout the initiative too fast and too wide. The organization cannot handle that amount of change and, as importantly, it has not yet learned how to change or what to change. This situation is addressed through the use of the tool called the Laminated Map.

Briefly, this use entails managers marking off all departments on a laminated map of the facility and then deciding which areas to say yes to (where to implement first) and which to postpone (where to implement later). In this way, management can regulate the flow of resources, focus on achieving a showcase (a vision place, internal to the facility) on key value-add areas, and prepare for an easier conversion during the second cycle, after some learning is in place.

Six: An Established Improvement Time Policy. A company that has switched to lean manufacturing runs a tight production schedule. A company that has not yet switched also runs full tilt—but for other reasons. If either company does not establish an official improvement time policy, very little improvement will ever happen in that enterprise.

In the battle between production time and improvement time, production will always win out. But without an established improvement time policy, there is a danger that needed improvement will never happen. It will certainly never turn into a habit if we simply leave improvement to the willing—those quiet, dedicated heroes who see the vision burning brightly before them and are determined to find a way.

When they succeed, in the absence of a clearly defined improvement time policy, these Rowers unintentionally send the message that separate time is not needed. Hats off to the executive who takes steps to establish such a policy nevertheless.

The lack of an established improvement time policy is one of the greatest corporate roadblocks to achieving a work culture rooted in continuous improvement.

For much more on an effective implementation startup, see Chapter 3 of my book, *Visual Systems: Harnessing the Power of a Visual Workplace.*

QMI ▌Visual-Lean® Institute

Gwendolyn Galsworth began researching and developing the principles, models, methods, and frameworks of workplace visuality over 25 years ago. In 1991, she formed Quality Methods International (QMI) to continue that work, and, more recently, the Visual-Lean® Institute in order to share the resulting wealth of knowledge and know-how, principles and methods.

QMI sets the pace for the industry. Our licensed affiliates are found in the United States, Canada, Mexico, Europe, India, and Australia. With over 20,000 actual visual solutions in our current database, we are continually refining and augmenting our system of instructional materials and designs. In our public seminars, QMI is honored to count the Shingo Prize, APICS, SME, Learning and Productivity, and AME as partners.

We can help you successfully implement the technologies of the Visual Workplace—assessing, diagnosing, and training your workforce and in-house trainers, coaching your leadership, and offering continuing support and consultation. Customized visual templates and implementation training are our specialty.

We offer a full range of self-transforming products, including videos/DVDs, books, tools, training aids, and complete off-the-shelf training packages if you prefer to achieve visuality on your own.

Whether your company is a factory, forge, truck fleet, mine, hospital, school, office or bank—and whether directly with us, our affiliates or on your own—QMI can help you acquire the knowledge, know-how, inspiration, and confidence you need to convert your organization into a fully-functioning visual enterprise that leaps forward into excellence through visual solutions.

QMI Books and Manuals

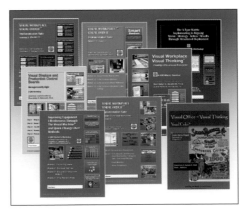

Visual Workplace-Visual Order DVD Training System (with Spanish subtitles)

Training of Trainers at the Visual-Lean® Institute

Track	Track Content/Courses	
Track 1	Visual Workplace/Visual Thinking Briefing + Pre-Launch Planning	
Track 2	Visual Order/Visual Inventiveness Suite	
Track 3	Becoming a Leader of Improvement (1): New Role for Supervisors & Managers	Management by Sight: Visual Displays/Control Boards
Track 4	The Visual Machine® Suite	Machine Lubrication: Visual & Effective
Track 5	Becoming a Leader of improvement (2): Creating a Business Systems Template	Policy Deployment + Operations Road Map
Track 6	The Visual-Lean® Office Suite	
Track 7	Becoming a Leader of Improvement (3): Visual Metrics/Visual Results	Visual Problem-Solving Visual Standard-Making
Track 8	Visual Adherence: Visual Standards/Visual Controls	Achieving Zero Defects: Visual Guarantees (Poka-Yoke)

QMI/Visual-Lean® Institute Curriculum

Webinars

Keynotes

 **Conferences**

Public Seminars

Visual Benchmarking Tours

Training Aides and Tools

Photo Albums, CDs, Wall Charts, Audio Lecture CDs, Tool Kits: Exercises and Checklist

On-Site Assessments and Implementations

Resource Section

> *In nearly 25 years in the field of manufacturing improvement, I have been privileged to meet and work with the providers of other critical services, linked to visual conversions. In this section of the Appendix, I describe several of them and invite you to consider ways each might help you on your own visual-lean journey to excellence.* **—Gwendolyn**

Don Guild and Synchronous Management

Because the high volume/low mix world of automotive manufacturing served as the model for most lean production methods, companies with lower volume/higher mix requirements are often challenged to find lean coaching services that serve their unique kanban/pull system needs. In addition, many firms offering lean on-site services rely heavily on the Kaizen Blitz (event-based) format to implement this change. While the blitz approach has many merits, it is not the only available method; in some cases, it is not the preferred one.

I have known the work of Don Guild and his company, Synchronous Management, for over 20 years and find them both remarkable. With over 40 years in manufacturing including 20 in the field of manufacturing improvement, Don and his team deliver insightful instruction and consultation in the principles and practices of pull for any ratio of volume and mix—as well as exceptional hands-on technical expertise in quantifying kanban and supermarket levels, required for success in this efforts. And visuality is part and parcel of Don's approach.

Every company who makes pull/kanban a part of its lean strategy struggles with two issues. First, how do we right-size inventories to get the best possible flow? And, how do we make sure kanban sizes are adjusted as product structures, manufacturing processes, and customer demands change? Wrong-sizing kanbans means resources are too often engaged in producing what we do not need, and not available to produce what we do need. The expediting and firefighting continue, and inventory levels remain high—even with kanban!

Second, how best do we signal replenishment? Do we use empty containers, kanban cards, first-in-first-out lanes, min/max, or some other technique? Too often, cumbersome manual techniques cause the pull system to deteriorate for lack of maintenance or to be limited in scope to only a few products. We spend too much non-value adding time making—and remaking—kanban cards. Visual does not have to mean manual! Each supermarket's visual signaling method must be appropriate to its supplier—and must be sustainable. No one approach fits all.

Synchronous Management provides solutions to all of these issues. We show you how to harvest data which resides in every automated Material Requirements Planning system so you can size and resize your supermarkets with ease. And we do it without proprietary software.

Then we help you select both manual and automated visual pull techniques—and to know when each is applicable. You can then understand the effects of your own management policies on your ability to implement and maintain an effective system for controlling and improving material flow.

Don Guild, Principal
Synchronous Management
51 Seaside Avenue
Milford, Connecticut 06460

Phone: 203-877-1287
Email: info@synchronousmanagement.com
Website: www.synchronousmanagement.com

DuraStripe and Arthur Rock Associates

In my experience, borders are the single most powerful device for establishing the *visual where*—the foundation of the visual workplace.

Yet, there are two great challenges in this. The first is getting borders to stick, especially in heavy forklift traffic or where floors are old, bruised, and beaten. The second is being able to remove a border quickly when the pattern of the flow changes, as it regularly does in a lean rollout. Some companies accomplished the first challenge by applying two coats of paint (each cured) to a very clean surface, followed by two coats of sealant. Such borders can last a year or more. But then what do you do when the flow changes—and then changes again? A new solution is needed.

At last there is one: DuraStripe, a flexible bordering system, distributed by Arthur Rock.

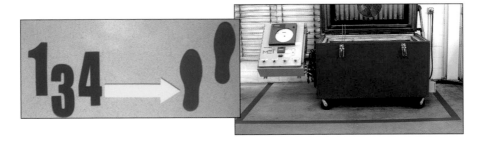

DuraStripe®* is a two-ply product of PVC and adhesive that requires no cure time to install. Just peel and stick. DuraStripe stands up exceptionally well to fork lift traffic,**pallet jacks, and industrial floor scrubbers. In addition, it can be removed by hand and leaves little or no residue.

DuraStripe also comes in letters and numbers—as well as pux (3.5" dots), corners, arrows, and other shapes that allow for lots of flexibility and are perfect for uneven surfaces, non-linear configurations, and high-hit zones. *Extreme DuraStripe*, a specialty product, works well in standing water, such as on exposed loading docks. Other DuraStripe versions are suitable for use in most food-processing, medical, and clean room environments. With a two-year warranty, DuraStripe is available in rolls of 2", 3", 4", and 6" widths and comes in seven primary colors (each roll holds 100 feet).

Established in 1976, Arthur Rock Associates, Inc. is a distributor of DuraStripe, static control, material handling, packaging, and ergonomic products, including mats for the aluminum industry. DuraStripe is one of its newest and most popular products because it is so easy to install and maintain and is ideal for customizing unique flow patterns in the visual-lean^{sm} enterprise.

Clients include Applied Medical, Boston Scientific, Cardinal Health, Northrop Grumman, General Atomics, General Dynamics, Hewlett-Packard, Guidant Corporation, Kyocera, Parker Hannifin, QUALCOMM, and SAIC.

To request a brochure, samples or discounted pricing, contact Connie Rock.

Phone: 858-755-4703
Email: Connie@arthurrock.com
Website: www.arthurrock.com

---

* DuraStripe is a registered trademark of Ergomat LLC.
** Of course, anyone who wants to cause damage to DuraStripe, can—for example, by pushing and dragging pallets or spinning forklift wheels directly on the border.

Rent Your Own In-House Sign Shop

The visual workplace is a physical workplace. Vital information gets translated into actual visual devices and mini-systems, like the ones in this book. While most visual devices are extremely low-cost, a company can incur sizeable direct expenses for professionally-made signage and boards, especially if the facility is a large one.

Visual Workplace LLC now offers an alternative that allows you to make your own visuals quickly, easily, and at a fraction of the cost of using an outside source: your own *In-House Sign Shop*. No more waiting for an estimate from an outside source, for approval to order a sign or for delivery.

You won't *Get Lean...*
Until you *Get Visual!*

Visual Workplace®, LLC rents sign-making systems for $99/month—called the In-House Sign Shop—that enable you to create a range of visual devices for your lean and visual factory rollout.

Included in your Sign Shop is: a Sign Plotter (similar to a CAD plotter); special software specific to sign applications; and on-site training to show you how to use the system. Your In-House Sign Shop also contains the Idea Book and CD, with photographs and over 500 editable visual device templates benchmarked from some of the best visual factories in the country.

Your In-House Sign Shop enables you to establish, maintain, and update your visual solutions, even when your process changes (see illustration).

After your training, you then purchase your supplies from Visual Workplace, LLC. Now you and your company have the ability to create product and inventory control boards, dry erase boards, any type of address and labeling material in a range of sizes and colors, shadow boards for tools, work instructions boards (e.g., for quality, kanban, safety), and so on.

Our research shows that companies with their own In-House Sign Shop can save up to 75% of what it could cost to purchase these same devices from an outside source.

The possibilities are endless. Rentals are month-to-month. For more information, contact Rhonda Kovera.

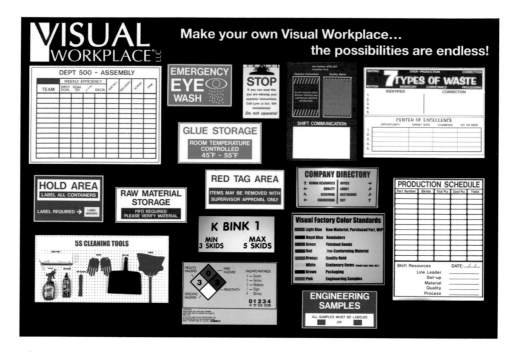

Phone: 877-523-4088 (toll free)

Phone: 616-662-0307 (direct)

Email: info@visual-work-place.com

Website: www.visual-work-place.com

Brady Corporation
A Leading Supplier of Facility ID and Visual Workplace Solutions

Brady is known globally for just the kind of workplace identification products that many of you use in the early stages of your journey to workplace visuality.

We've used their portable HandiMark label makers in many Visual Blitzes. As the name indicates, it's handy and does a great job. Check out their desktop printing systems that make your visuals look like the work of a professional graphics shop.

As many of you know, I am a great believer in the use of hand-made signs and workplace art. But, of course, there's always room for the kind of quick, durable, print-quality visuals that Brady can provide! Check Brady out on the web (www.bradyid.com/visualworkplace). You'll find lots of useful ideas and really great products.

Create Lean Visuals On-Site and On-Demand
Make your own 5S tags and labels, kanban cards, gauge indicators, visual displays and more using Brady's visual workplace printing systems.

Brady's Wide Range of Solutions

Brady systems are composed of software, printers and media specially designed for use in industrial environments. The thermal-transfer printed output withstands abrasion, moisture, sun, plus many common chemicals and cleansers. In addition the adhesive label material sticks and stays stuck to a wide variety of surfaces, including pipes, walls, pegboard, floors, etc.

	GlobalMark® 2 Industrial Labeler	PowerMark™ Sign & Labeler	MiniMark™ Industrial Labeler	HandiMark® Portable Labeler	IDXPERT™ Handheld Labeler	ID PAL™ Labeling Tool
Tape Width	$^1/_2$" - 4"	4" - 10"	$^1/_2$" - 4"	$^3/_8$" - 2"	$^1/_2$"-1$^1/_2$"	$^3/_8$" - $^3/_4$"
Built-in Display w/ keyboard	Yes	Yes	No	Yes	Yes	Yes
PC Connectivity	Yes	Yes	Yes	Yes	Yes	No
Plotter (cuts text/shapes)	Yes (Color & Cut only)	No	No	No	No	No
Color	Multiple spot colors and process color	Multiple spot color	Single spot color	Single spot color	Single spot color	Single spot color
Media Types	Indoor / outdoor vinyl, repositionable vinyl, poly tag stock, magnetic, reflective, phosphorescent, tamper resistant, metalized polyester, and more.	Indoor / outdoor vinyl, polyester tag stock, reflective, phosphorescent, polyester and more.	Indoor / outdoor vinyl, tamper resistant, and more.	Indoor / outdoor vinyl, repositionable vinyl, economy polyester, reflective, tamper resistant	Indoor / outdoor vinyl, plus wide variety of specialty materials including diecuts for electrical and datacommunications marking	Vinyl, plus nylon cloth and polyester for wire and cable marking

GlobalMark—It's more than just a label maker!

Tags and Kanban Cards
Print to flexible polyester tag stock or apply adhesive labels to rigid cards

Large Signs and Placards
Cutout text and apply to sign or placard material

Magnets
Print directly to magnetic material or cut adhesive labels to fit your own magnets

Paint Stencils
Cut characters on repositionable vinyl sticks but is easy to peel off

BRADY
WHEN PERFORMANCE MATTERS MOST™

Management Resource Plus (MRPlus)

One day I got a long letter from Oscar Roche, an improvement specialist from "down under." Oscar had read the book you have in hand (first edition), was full of insight and enthusiasm for workplace visuality, and asked how he could learn more and bring our methods to his clients. The rest, as they say, is history.

Management Resource Plus (MRPlus) is a licensed affiliate of QMI/Visual-Lean® Institute, trained to help companies throughout Australia and Asia stay locally and globally competitive through QMI's visual workplace technologies.

MRPlus Director and founder Oscar Roche, and his team of certified QMI trainers, use visual systems as a vital component of their project-based learning approach to mentoring companies as they "build the house of Visual-Lean."

Client companies such as DeBortoli Wines, Orlando Wines (makers of the famous Jacobs Creek brand), Casella Wines (home of the Yellow Tail brand), Markerry Industries, Gannon Vietnam, and Tetra Pak (Vietnam) have all benefited significantly from the delivery of Visual Workplace seminar, workshops, and facilitation. All recognize the power of workplace visuality for embedding the process of continuous improvement into the organization and as a vehicle for their journey to enterprise excellence.

Visuality has been revolutionary in the complex market environment of SE Asia. With their great diversity of language and culture, those companies have come to understand the power of visual solutions to embed the details of work in nonverbal forms into the physical environment. The entire company then becomes a gigantic adherence mechanism.

If you are a traditional manufacturer, MRPlus will help you optimize your existing approach. If you are already on the journey to Lean, we will help extend and support your Lean conversion and make those gains sustainable.

Visual Workplace Australasia (Management Resource Plus)
Phone: 0427 066348 (61 427 066348)
Fax: 02 692 6689 (61 2 69626689)
Website: www.mrplus.com.au

Oscar Roche   Ben Chopping

Sherrie Ford and the Transformation of the Work Culture

I had the extreme pleasure of coming to know the work of Dr. Sherrie Ford several years ago, quite by coincidence. You can imagine my pleasure and surprise at noticing the deep parallels between her work and mine.

I do not think I have ever met a person more dedicated than Dr. Ford to the conversion of work culture and the upliftment of the company through a deep and abiding change in both an organization's power structure and the dynamic relationships between the people who work there, across all functions.

Sherrie embodies the values and principles she teaches with a profound reverence for the individual. Yet she is also passionately committed to making companies financially secure and prosperous. She is one of our nation's pre-eminent thought leaders and culture authority. I am honored to know her and her business partner, Steve Hollis.

Ever the supporters of the local economy and the highest of work culture values, Sherrie and Steve have recently become co-owners of PowerPartners, a vertically-integrated transformer manufacturer in Athens, Georgia—even as they continue their consulting work with other companies.

Change Partners (CP), a consulting firm in Athens, Georgia, provides work culture solutions for world-class, high-performance-oriented companies. Its strength is effective organizational change-management strategies that respond to the escalating needs of clients.

CP offers on-site seminars and complete implementations, working primarily with clients in manufacturing who are ready to become culture makers first—recognizing excellence in leadership, communication, and training as the strategic drivers that lead to dramatic and lasting improvements in quality, machine uptime, speed to market, innovations, and wage/benefit approaches. This is not event-based change. It is a thorough and meticulous re-configuration and release of the riches of the work culture that results in long life and prosperity for the enterprise and the community within which it exists.

Change Partners, LLC
220 College Avenue, Suite 444
Athens, Georgia 30601

Phone: 706-546-4045
Fax: 706-546-1686
Website: www.changepartners.com

The Shingo Prize for Manufacturing Excellence

Every company that commits to excellence requires a roadmap to get there. The roadmap for the lean side of the conversion is comprehensively provided by the Shingo Prize, our national prize for manufacturing.

Whether you plan to challenge for the Prize or not, if you want to understand concrete ways to improve your operations, there is no better diagnostic format I can recommend than the Shingo Prize model and the application criteria it includes. You can download these directly from: www.shingoprize.org

Named after Dr. Shigeo Shingo, co-architect of the Toyota Production System, the *Shingo Prize for Operational Excellence* recognizes companies in North America that have demonstrated outstanding achievements in manufacturing processing, quality enhancement, productivity improvement, and customer satisfaction.

Established in 1988, the Prize promotes awareness of Lean manufacturing concepts as well as the premise that world-class business performance may be achieved through focused improvements in core manufacturing and business processes. In 2009, the Prize will confer a special award in the area of workplace visuality called, *The Visual Workplace Medallion*. Dr. Galsworth has been asked to organize this.

The Shingo Prize recognizes organizations and research, consistent with its philosophy and guidelines, in three award categories:

Robert D. Miller, Executive Director
Shingo Prize
3521 Old Main Hill
Utah State University
Logan, Utah 84322-3521
Website: www.shingoprize.org
Phone: 435-797-2279
Fax: 435-797-3440

• **Business Prize:** recognizes companies in the private sector that demonstrate the use of world-class operational strategies and practices to achieve world-class results.

• **Public Sector Prize:** recognizes organizations in the public sector/government-owned facilities that demonstrate the use of world-class operational strategies and practices to achieve world-class results.

• **Research Prize:** recognizes research and writing regarding new knowledge and understanding in the field.

Every year over one hundred Shingo Board Examiners review the Achievement Reports of the companies that challenge for the Prize and then visit qualifying companies to validate such achievements. Annual recipients who are chosen from that second group are honored at the Shingo Prize Annual Conference.

On-The-Job Training Through Visual SOPs

As an advocate for mechanical visual solutions, I prefer visual devices that physically exist in the flow of work. Yet there are alternatives worth our attention. Visual standards in an electronic format is one of them.

I came across the work of Expert-OJT in my search for a better way for companies to document, catalogue, verify, and refine their formal and information standard operating procedures (SOPs). The computer-based methodology known as Expert-OJT is exceedingly useful for this purpose.

Since 1982, Expert OJT has been a leader in structured on-the-job training and visual job aids. At the heart of the E-OJT process is documenting, refining, validating, and publishing the organization's standard operating procedures (SOPs). In the process, your own team learns to use the Expert-OJT system, including how to use visual job aids in training the workforce.

Using a series of templates that streamline and standardize your SOPs, your Expert-OJT instructor makes sure the team you chose to learn and apply this process, understands it and can apply the process thoroughly and independently once the instructor leaves your site.

Expert-OJT has demonstrated again and again that practically anyone can learn how to write visual aids and use them to train others on the job.

Dr. Jeffrey J. Nelson is founder/ president and principal developer of the Expert OJT System which has been used throughout the world in virtually every type of enterprise. Client companies include Boeing, Procter & Gamble, Allstate, Wyeth Labs, FEMA, Harley Davison, ExxonMobil and NC Dept of Labor.

Dr. Jeff Nelson
Expert-OJT
P.O. Box 12024
Newport News, Virginia 23612

Phone: 757-884-9333 (direct)
Toll Free: 888-658-2800 (U.S. only)
Fax: 757-884-9335
Website: www.expertojt.com

Suggested Reading

The Visual Workplace

Make No Mistake: An Outcome-Based Approach to Mistake-Proofing, Martin Hinckley (Productivity Press, 2001).

Poka Yoke: Improving Product Quality by Preventing Defects, edited by NKS/Factory Magazine (Productivity Press, 1988).

The New Standardization: Keystone of Continuous Improvement in Manufacturing, Shigehiro Nakamura (Productivity Press, 1993).

The Visual Factory: Building Participation through Shared Information, Michel Greif (Productivity Press, 1991).

Visual Systems for Improving Equipment Effectiveness, Robert L. Williamson (Strategic Work Systems Press, 1998).

Visual Systems: Harnessing the Power of a Visual Workplace, Gwendolyn D. Galsworth (Amacom, 1997).

*Visual Workplace Visual Order*sm *Associate Handbook*, Gwendolyn D. Galsworth (Visual-Lean Enterprise Press, 1999).

Zero Quality Control: Source Inspection and the Poka-Yoke System, Shigeo Shingo (Productivity Press, 1986).

Lean and Time-Based Production Systems

A Study of the Toyota Production System: From an Industrial Engineering Viewpoint, Shigeo Shingo (Productivity Press, 1989).

Implementing a Lean Management System, Thomas L. Jackson (Productivity Press, 1997).

Japanese Manufacturing Techniques: Nine Lessons in Simplicity, Richard J. Schonberger (The Free Press, 1982).

Just-In-Time for America: A Common Sense Production Strategy, Kenneth A. Wantuck (KWA Media, 1989).

Kaikaku: The Power and Magic of Lean, Norman Bodek (PCS Press, 2004).

Kanban/Just-In-Time at Toyota: Management Begins at the Workplace, edited by Japan Management Association (Productivity Press, 1986).

Lean Thinking: Banish Waste and Create Wealth in Your Corporation, James P. Womack (Simon & Schuster, 1996).

Let's Fix It! Overcoming the Crisis in Manufacturing, Richard J. Schonberger (The Free Press, 2001).

One-Piece Flow: Cell Design for Transforming the Production Process, Kenichi Sekine (Productivity Press, 1992).

Quantum Leap: In Speed to Market, John R. Costanza (JIT Institute of Technology, 1989).

Revolution in Manufacturing: The SMED System, Shigeo Shingo (Productivity Press, 1985).

Smart, Simple Design: Using Variety Effectiveness to Reduce Total Cost and Maximize Customer Selection, Gwendolyn D. Galsworth (John Wiley & Sons, 1994).

The Goal: Excellence in Manufacturing, Eliyahu M. Goldratt and Jeff Cox (North River Press, 1984).

TPM Development Program: Implementing Total Productive Maintenance, Seiichi Nakajima (Productivity Press, 1989).

Organizational Development and Work Culture

Building Organizational Fitness: Management Methodology for Transformation and Strategic Advantage, Ryuji Fukuda (Productivity Press, 1997).

Caught in the Middle: A Leadership Guide for Partnership in the Workplace, Rick Maurer (Productivity Press, 1989).

CEDAC: A Tool for Continuous Systematic Improvement, Ryuji Fukuda (Productivity Press, 1996).

Keys to Workplace Improvement, Iwao Kobayashi (Productivity Press, 1990).

Managerial Engineering, Ryuji Fukuda (Productivity Press, 1983).

Profits Beyond Measure: Extraordinary Results Through Attention to Work and People, H. Thomas Johnson (The Free Press, 2000).

Relevance Regained: From Top-Down Control to Bottom-Up Empowerment, H. Thomas Johnson (The Free Press, 1992).

Servant Leadership: A Journey into the Nature of Legitimate Power and Greatness, Robert K. Greenleaf (Paulist Press, 1997).

The Soul of the Enterprise: Creating a Dynamic Vision for American Manufacturing, Robert Hall (John Wiley & Sons, 1993).

Other

Chaos: Making a New Science, James Gleick (Viking Penguin).

Feng Shui: The Chinese Art of Placement, Sarah Rossbach (Arcana, 1983).

Seven Experiments That Could Change the World, Rupert Sheldrake (River Books, 1995).

The Chrysanthemum and the Sword, Ruth Benedict (Houghton-Mifflin, 1989).

The Design of Everyday Things, Donald Norman (Doubleday, New York, 1988).

When Elephants Weep: The Emotional Lives of Animals, Jeffrey Moussaieff Masson and Susan McCarthy (Bantam, 1995).

Will I Be the Hero of My Own Life?, Swami Chetanananda (Rudra Press, 1995).

Your Garagenous Zone: Innovative Ideas for the Garage, Bill West (Paragon Garage Company, 2004).

INDEX

4Ws + 2Hs, 52
5S+1 Visual Order®, 101-127, 129
Alvarado, Angie, 72-77
Alvez, Ed, 113
Antunes, Bill, 90
Automatic recoil, 70, 82, 89, 116-7, 129
Azar, Salam, 113

Balanced Scorecard, 140, 143
Barter, Cindy, 35
Benedictus, Paulette, 46, 47
Biggest mistake, 70-72
Bottom-up paradigm, 58-59
Bowersmith, Sheila, 108
Building blocks of visual thinking, 6, 21-52
Bushmich, Kenny, 50

Catatao, Luis, 34, 162
Caught in the middle, 63
CEDAC, 150
Chetanananda, Swami, 98
Collective intelligence/consciousness
    of enterprise, 187
Color coding, 115, 117, 120, 160, 168, 170

Comeau, Bob, 117
Command and control model, 57-59
Context visuals, 187-190, 191
Could-Be Map, 111
Critical path, 7, 186-7
Critical path visuals, 188-9
Culture alignment, 16-7
Culture conversion, 53
Customer-driven visual order, 122-5, 124-5
Cycle of visual thinking, 48-49

David Copperfield, 79
Decoupling, 195
DeLeon, Carlos, 154
Delphi Automotive, 35, 117, 132
Delphi Rimir, 141, 157, 159-60, 177
Deltronicos, 34, 138, 143-4
Design-to-task, 153, 155, 156
Dilbert, 8,
Dominance hierarchy, 87
DuraStripe, 115, 127

Eight building blocks of visual
    thinking, 6, 21-52

221

Eight deadly wastes vs motion, 41
Einstein, Albert, 64, 110
Ell, Rick, 117
Empowerment, 57, 64-72, 192-93
Evolution of the "I", 83-85, 92-94
Exam-awards process, 174-6
Expert-OJT, 150

False decision point, 59-63
First question is free rule, 37
First S is for Spirit, 106
Fleet Engineers, 12, 34
Four types of visual devices, 13,14
France, Tyler 113
Freudenberg-NOK, 158
Fukuda, Ryuji, 10, 11, 98, 145, 150

Geertruida, Victor, 19
Governance, 57
Griggs, Robin, 96

Hamilton, Bruce, 97, 177
Hank's story, 24-27
Harris Corp., 116,125
Heijink, Jean, 124
Heijunka, 157,158, 186
Hidden geometry, 64-66
Hinckley, Martin, 177
Holetz, Brenda, 139
Hop, Henk, 137

Identity evolution, process of, 80-81
I-driven, 22-30, 81, 82, 87-93, 95-97
Implementation pathway, 99
Information deficits, 15-16, 36, 43
Information hoarding, 42
ISO, 33

Jackson, Tom, 150
Janssen, Max, 19

Johnson, Eric, 154
Johnson, Thomas, 150
Jones, Daniel T, 195

Kaizen blitz, 69, 74
Kanban, 96, 155, 157, 158, 186
Kaplan, Robert S., 150

Lead team, 115, 127
Lean, purpose of, 181-2, 183-4
Lockheed-Martin (LM-Aero), 156
Lopuszynski, Frank, 73
Love, April, 113
Low-hanging fruit, 71

Macro-visual environment, 171,174
Meditation, 118
Midwest Regional Medical Center, 156
Min/max, 155
Mind, as pattern seeking mechanism, 115-21
Mooren, Piet, 124
Motion, 38-44
Motion metric, 47-48
Motion, what it is not, 39
Moving too quickly to teams, 85-87
Muda, 43
Mulder, Frank, 136-7

Need to know (NTK), 22-30, 81-82, 72
Need to share (NTS), 22-30, 81-82
New culture, 56
New enterprise, 20
Norton, David P., 150
Non-value-adding activity,
    (NVA), 43, 44, 148
Nooteboom, Henk, 18

Ohno, Taiichi, 129

Pacheco, John, 91

Packard Electric (Rio Bravo IV), 146
Parker Denison, 108, 117, 118, 120, 126
Parker Hannifin, 152-3
Participation myths, 66-70
Pattern of work, 115-121
Picard, Capt. Jean-Luc, 44
Plymouth Tube, 96, 146
Podolski, Bill, 126
Poka-yoke, 159-163, 177
Pollard, Stephen, 20, 192
Potted palm, 108-109
Power pyramids, 57-66
Pratt-Whitney, 148
Procedural standard, 31-32
Production control boards, 133-7
Pro-Life, Pro-Choice, 61-62

QCO, 165
Questions, unasked, 22

Red tagging, 105, 173
Results, bottom line, 9, 112-3, 167, 182, 185, 192
Right angles cause motion, 126
Robins, Paula, 148
Rolls-Royce plc, 20, 116, 139, 150, 156, 162, 182
Rowers, watchers and grumblers, 93-95
Royal Nooteboom Trailers, 18-19, 124, 136-7, 148
Russel, Paul, 113

S1 stories, 108-9
S1/Sort, 105-109
S2/Shine, 107, 110, 112-113
S3/Secure Safety, 110, 112-113
S4/Select Locations, 56, 110-111, 114
S5/Set Locations, 111, 114-121
Santos, Bernice, 46
ScoreBoard process, 147, 148

Sears, 73-77, 139, 173
Seiri, etc. (Japanese 5S), 102
Seton ID Products, 35, 152-3, 154
Sherman, Aleta, 101, 104
Shingo Prize, 195
Shingo, Shigeo, 163, 165, 177, 195
Six core questions, 33-36
Skyworks Solutions, 45, 50, 51, 124
Slanty borders, 126
Smart placement, 76, 110
Smart Simple Design, 97
SOPs, 131-2
Sparrows, Melody, 116
Standard, Dr. Fukuda's definition of, 145
Standards, 30-33
Startup requirements, 127, appendix
Sustainability, 9, 182, 192

Technical standard, 30-31
Technologies of the visual workplace, 1, 17, 53, 55-56, 99-100, 182
Ted's story, 80
Ten doorways into workplace visuality, 100, 130, 165
Territorial imperative, 106
The Will, 88-89, 94-95
Theiss, Ken, 108
Toyota Production System (TPS), 41, 129, 193, 195
TPM, 167
Traditional culture, 56
Traffic-light pull, 157-9, 160
Trailmobile/Canada, 112-113, 116, 132
Two pyramids of power, 57-70
Two wings of a bird, 1, 9, 53, 181

United Electric Controls, 34, 35, 90-1, 117,162

Value field, 44-47, 50,51

van Uden, Toon, 136
Visual controls, 1-9, 3, 151, 152, 154
Visual controls, pull systems, 155, 159, 186
Visual displays, 133-9
Visual guarantees, 151, 159-63, 177
Visual-Lean® Alliance, 9, 18, 176, 179,
    181-195
Visual-Lean® Office, 168-173
Visual Machine®, 166-168, 164
Visual metrics, 140-4
Visual order, 101-127, 129
Visual problem-solving, 145-9
Visual, purpose of, 182, 184-6
Visual standards, 13, 131-33
Visual thinker, thinking, 2, 18, 21, 193
Visual where, 34, 70-72, 81-82, 88-9,
    114-121, 150
Visual workplace, definition, 3, 10
Voogt, Berry, 19

Walls, Dorothy, 108
Waste, 43
Weak-I, 83-93
What-Is Map, 111, 127
Wiremold, 146, 158
Wiseman, Tom, 112
Womack, James, 195
Work, definition, 44
Work culture, definition, 55
    need for new paradigm in, 56
    people worth the pause in, 95-97

X-Type Matrix, 150

Yu, Annie, 50

Zero Quality Control, 165

NOTES

NOTES